THE
POSSIBLE
SELF

A LEADER'S GUIDE TO
PERSONAL DEVELOPMENT

MAJA DJIKIC

Berrett–Koehler Publishers, Inc.

For my mother and father, Nermana and Mugdim

Berrett-Koehler Publishers, Inc.
1333 Broadway, Suite 1000
Oakland, CA 94612-1921
Tel: (510) 817-2277
Fax: (510) 817-2278
www.bkconnection.com

ORDERING INFORMATION

Quantity sales. Special discounts are available on quantity purchases by corporations, associations, and others. For details, contact the "Special Sales Department" at the Berrett-Koehler address above.
Individual sales. Berrett-Koehler publications are available through most bookstores. They can also be ordered directly from Berrett-Koehler: Tel: (800) 929–2929; Fax: (802) 864–7626; www.bkconnection.com.
Orders for college textbook / course adoption use. Please contact Berrett-Koehler: Tel: (800) 929–2929; Fax: (802) 864–7626.

Distributed to the U.S. trade and internationally by Penguin Random House Publisher Services.

Berrett-Koehler and the BK logo are registered trademarks of Berrett-Koehler Publishers, Inc.

Printed in the United States of America

Berrett-Koehler books are printed on long-lasting acid-free paper. When it is available, we choose paper that has been manufactured by environmentally responsible processes. These may include using trees grown in sustainable forests, incorporating recycled paper, minimizing chlorine in bleaching, or recycling the energy produced at the paper mill.

Library of Congress Cataloging-in-Publication Data
Names: Djikic, Maja, author.
Title: The possible self : a leader's guide to personal development / Maja Djikic.
Description: First edition. | Oakland, CA : Berrett-Koehler Publishers, Inc., [2024] |
    Includes bibliographical references and index.
Identifiers: LCCN 2023038055 (print) | LCCN 2023038056 (ebook) |
    ISBN 9781523006014 (paperback) | ISBN 9781523006021 (pdf) |
    ISBN 9781523006038 (epub)
Subjects: LCSH: Self-actualization (Psychology) | Self-realization. | Leadership.
Classification: LCC BF637.S4 D58 2024 (print) | LCC BF637.S4 (ebook) |
    DDC 158.1—dc23/eng/20231117
LC record available at https://lccn.loc.gov/2023038055
LC ebook record available at https://lccn.loc.gov/2023038056

First Edition

30 29 28 27 26 25 24 23   10 9 8 7 6 5 4 3 2 1

Book production: Westchester Publishing Services
Cover design: Adam Johnson

CONTENTS

PART III   The Wheel in Motion

INTRODUCTION

Between Our First and Last Breath

Development—a natural process that makes living beings grow over time into possible future selves—is a hallmark of all life. When it works well, it does so seamlessly. It's difficult not to be impressed by the process that turns earthy bulbs into flowers and helpless infants into speaking beings. Yet what seems so simple for flowers and infants is far more complicated for adults. The very process that propels life toward its potential can slow, or sometimes stop.

Development is possible throughout our lifetime, until our very last breath. As adults, though, we find that this same force that is supposed to move us to our potential can stall. While we may have times of rapid development, we can also experience plateaus in our growth where we remain in stagnation, sometimes for years. When we encounter a seemingly intractable problem in some domain of our life and try to change—to stop overworking, to find self-confidence, to cultivate better relationships, or to become better leaders—we can find ourselves at a loss. What makes us stuck? Why can't we change? And should we even keep trying? The battle for self-change is often grueling and painful, and we may want to give up, but giving up the struggle feels like abandoning the person we could become, our possible self.

As a personality psychologist teaching in a school of management, every day I encounter professionals who, despite their accomplishments, feel stalled in some domain of their life. They have tried, many times and in many ways, to change the part of themselves that keeps them back, without a lasting success. Often they are on the verge of giving up and accepting their limitation as "who they are." This book is my call to them to not give up. It is also my answer to their questions: What is the self? How does self-development work, and why? What makes it go fast or slow? And why does it fail so often for so many of us? The book is written not just to inform but to help transform—with techniques that we can use to get unstuck and create a lasting change in our lives.

The central premise of this book is that no matter how long we have been stuck and how hard we have struggled to change, we can get unstuck and keep growing. But before I explain how this process works, it's important to address a counter-assumption that lurks in the background and negates the very premise of lifelong development—a corrosive suspicion that adults can't really change who they "are." It is this assumption that can make us want to give up on self-development, so it's important to ask ourselves where it comes from and how true it is.

ARE WE "SET LIKE PLASTER"?

One way we start believing that people don't change is by looking around. After all, many around us don't change, no matter how much they try: friends who are always on a diet, spouses consumed by anger, people repeating relationship mistakes, uncoachable bosses. We can also spend years of our lives trying to change some part of ourselves without success. It's natural that we may start believing this is just "who we are." And up until the beginning of this century, scientists would have agreed with us.

"Set like plaster" is how some researchers have described personality as recently as the 1990s.[1] Personality traits—stable ways in which we interact with ourselves and others—were supposed to be set into an unchangeable form by age 30. Traits were considered "hardwired"— genetically determined and therefore immune to change. If, as adults, we encountered a problem, we were supposed to focus on changing problematic behaviors. The idea was that while the trait (who we "are") couldn't change, we could use our willpower to change our behaviors and try to keep them steady, usually through habits.

The outcome of this way of looking at adult development was a proliferation of personality tests ($2 billion worth of them)[2] that are supposed to help us understand who we really are by identifying which "traits" we have and which "type" and "style" we belong to. In professional settings, we are often told to lean into our strengths because they're all we have, and we'd better make the best use of them to transcend our weaknesses. From this perspective, the message is clear: the plateau we reach in our life is our destination. We can try to fix behaviors as necessary, but there is nowhere else to go.

ESCAPING OUR BOXES

Given all this, why do we sometimes see change within and around us? We may have become less shy than we were during high school. We may observe friends who have become more stable or confident as they got older, or who underwent radical life transformations. People in our workplaces tell us we have "potential" and send us to workshops to develop our "soft skills." The premise that we can change is central to the work of many coaches, psychotherapists, counselors, psychologists, and other practitioners of personal development. Their insights align with the latest developments in personality and neuroscience research.

Over the last 20 years, researchers have shown that people's personality profiles continue to change throughout adulthood. For example, people tend to become more agreeable and conscientious as they age,[3] which makes sense given that, over time, we often gain social skills and are better able to control our impulses. The field of neuroplasticity has shown us that the brain can change itself, that it is plastic.[4] It means that so-called hardwired neural pathways can be rewired. This happens whenever stroke patients regain their speaking skills, when we acquire new habits, or when we sharpen our perception and memory as adults.[5] What seemed like a personality destination suddenly looks like a plateau at which we are resting before our next developmental climb.

But isn't our personality genetic? Not entirely. Genes give us a physiological predisposition called a temperament; for example, a higher sensitivity to sound or taste, or a fast reaction time to emotional stimuli. Our learned way of dealing with that temperament will result in a personality trait. While one person with higher sensitivity to sound may avoid contact with others and become shy, another, living in a family of musicians, may learn to use their heightened sensitivity to connect with others through music. *We can think of our personality traits as early skills in living with our temperament within our unique environments.* This means that, as adults, we can learn other ways of living with our predispositions and, therefore, grow our personality.

Instead of considering personality traits as our destinations, we can think of them as early inner skills, as temporary plateaus from which we continue to grow. Instead of seeing our undeveloped traits as boxes in which we had better get comfortable, we can leave them and develop parts of ourselves long left dormant. If we are emotionally unstable, we may seek to build emotional resilience; if we are chronically extroverted, we can learn to be comfortable in solitude. This is a true expansion of our way of being, not a willful and forced surface change in behavior while the rest of the self pulls us the other way. The feeling of being unfulfilled often comes from staying in our box and not exploring and developing our supposed weaknesses. We can leave our boxes and continue to grow, develop, and expand.

REIGNITING SELF-DEVELOPMENT

Knowing that we can change brings us to the central topic of this book: how do we change deeply without falling back into old ways of being? And why do we fail so often at what should come naturally—developing toward our possible self? Understanding why we fail so often will help us set up the right conditions for lasting self-growth.

One reason why we fail to change is that we often focus our attempts on our **behaviors**, the most visible and measurable parts of the self. Behaviors can be observed and counted, which gives us a quick reference point for our progress. But the self is not just our behaviors, it is also our **mind, emotions, motivations**, and past learnings carried in our **bodies**. These parts of the self are like spokes of a wheel that must act together if we want to move without breaking. When we act only on behaviors, it's as if we try to move one spoke one way while the rest of the wheel is pushing in the opposite direction.

Even when we expand our effort beyond just behavior, most of the self-change techniques available to us tend to focus only on a few parts of the self. For example, habit-building highlights behaviors and motivation; cognitive-behavioral therapy focuses on the mind, emotions, and behavior; and trauma-based therapy delves into emotions and memories carried in our bodies. *To activate the natural movement of development and produce lasting change, we need to activate all five parts of the self, at the same time.* To do that, we must know how each part of the self moves, what makes it get stuck, and what it would take to restart its momentum again.

At any particular time in our life, there are multitudes of unique, developing potentials in the self—physical, relational, intellectual, familial, romantic, creative, and so forth—and each has its own developmental "wheel" that moves with its own speed. Some race along, some move sluggishly, and others stopped moving long ago. In this book, I aim to help you identify the wheels of self that have stopped or slowed and help restart their movement again.

The models of self and self-development that follow are based on 13 years of research and teaching students and professionals at the Rotman School of Management at the University of Toronto. The stories you are about to read—of Abhinav, Kai, Emily, and Aisha— are based on narratives of participants in my workshops and classes who have used the methods in this book to reignite their development. Their personal details have been changed to protect their privacy.

PART I

THE WHEEL
OF SELF

CHAPTER ONE

WHEN THE WHEEL
STOPS TURNING

"Happy families are all alike; every unhappy family is unhappy in its own way." This is how Tolstoy begins his masterpiece *Anna Karenina*. For individuals, we could say the opposite: when joyful, we are all different, moving toward our potential in unique, unreplicable ways. When suffering, we are all alike. With the rest of humanity we feel stagnation; alternate between frantic action and paralysis; suffer frustration and anxiety, rumination and negative self-thoughts; and try hopelessly not to repeat our past failures. We are alike in our suffering because, while our potential and paths are unique, the symptoms of getting stuck appear universal.

Before we even begin to understand how stagnation happens and how we can leave it behind, we are faced with the big question: What is the self? Ever since Freud divided the self into id, ego, and superego, hundreds of psychologists, sociologists, neuroscientists, anthropologists, and other human-centered professionals have been giving their answers to that question. My own answer, presented in Figure 1.1, is based on observing which "parts" of the self (that recur across many different psychological theories) are most important to people attempting self-change. The model is meant not to

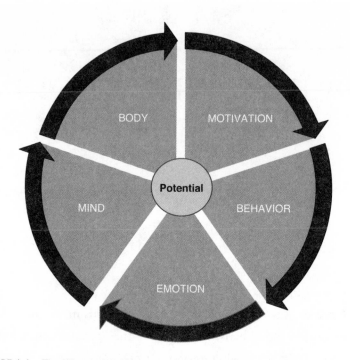

FIGURE 1.1   The Wheel of Self

be exhaustive but practical, something we can work with to restart our development.

One way to think of the self is as having five different parts, arranged here into a wheel: motivation, behavior, emotion, mind, and body (the last of which contains learnings from our past).

When most of us try to change (let's say reduce the number of doughnuts we eat each week), we often focus only on behavior. What we forget is that behavior is influenced by our motivation, that is, our wants and desires (for a delicious Boston cream doughnut), our emotions (the happiness we feel when we taste it), our thoughts (about how fluffy and creamy it will be), and by our body (that has been conditioned by many years of experience to expect a doughnut after lunch). Notice that behavior is governed by other parts of the self. This is why we need to study them in turn.

Just as kidneys, lungs, and intestines would be meaningless to study in isolation without considering an entire organism, so are parts of the self meaningless without understanding the self holistically. Yet just as a medical student would start by learning about different organ systems separately, we will learn (in Part II) what mechanisms govern these different parts of the self. But before that, let us see it in motion—when it moves well and when it stalls.

THE SELF IN ACTION

Imagine you are thinking of leaving your nine-to-five job as a project manager to start a freelancing career. You like the idea of being your own boss, collaborating on interesting projects, and having the flexibility to organize your life more meaningfully. To do this, it's not enough to change your circumstances. You also need to develop aspects of yourself that are needed for this life transition—how to be disciplined about time, develop confidence and interpersonal skills to offer your services to a wider network of clients, and know when to say no, to prevent burnout.

When the Wheel of Self is moving well, all five parts of the self are in harmonious, developmental motion. On the motivational side, you are driven by a curiosity about your subject matter and are inspired to devour materials that will lead you to your aim. Behaviorally, you seek out and explore articles, blogs, and books about freelancing and start connecting with people who are already working and living as you wish to do. The feeling of joy, an emotional signal of developmental movement, permeates your days, and you are excited and hopeful for what your future will bring. Your mind is drawn and attentive to anything to do with your new idea and will often get absorbed in reading articles or watching videos late into the night. Yet, despite the late nights and early mornings, your body feels easily energized, responsive, and restored (Figure 1.2).

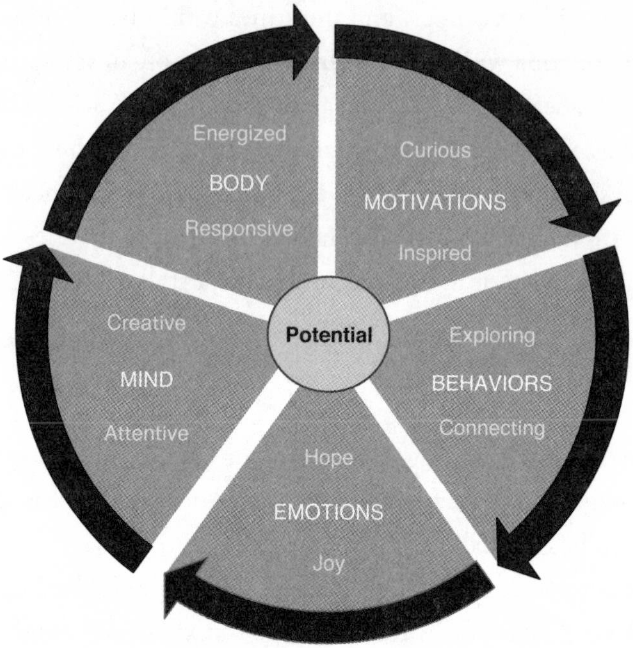

FIGURE 1.2 The Developing Self

When development is going well, all parts of the self work together, seamlessly supporting the change. When in the midst of this process, we don't have to try to change, apply willpower, or develop habits to keep our new behaviors. It happens organically, as if all parts of the self conspire to develop a new way of being. When the Wheel of Self is moving well, we don't try to develop, we simply do.

What happens when the Wheel of Self stalls? Abhinav, a 46-year-old physiotherapist, spent his 20-year career working too much. Now he had a full roster of clients and was a managing director of the clinic. He was heavily burdened with both clinical and administrative duties. Most evenings he would come home after his children had already been put to bed. During infrequent family vacations, he would get so anxious and desperate to continue work that more than once his wife suggested he return home early and at least let the children enjoy their few days on the beach. He knew his lifestyle was unhealthy and had tried to change, with no success.

With time, things got worse. He felt he was drifting away from his wife and was not as close to his two children as he wished to be. His health was deteriorating. His practice was full, yet he was still taking on additional patients on recommendation, particularly if they were elderly and had complex rehabilitation needs. In the previous decade, he had tried over and over again to cut down on his work, but his strategies to build new behavioral routines never seemed to work. His friends would tell him, "Just stop working that hard." Abhinav tried, of course, but his attempts left him feeling guilty, anxious, and broken.

Framing the problem of self-change as that of behavior change is a common misconception about self-transformation. We forget that behavior is influenced by all the other parts of the self: motivations, emotions, thoughts, and old patterns that we carry in our bodies. When we try to change behavior in one direction (trying to work less) while our minds, emotions, and bodies are fighting the opposite tendency (wanting to work more), what we are producing is not a self-change but a form of self-fragmentation. We have tried moving one part of the self while all other parts are stubbornly static or moving in the opposite direction. It is the kind of change that leaves us stressed, exhausted, and full of guilt once we revert to the old behavior. *For a successful and lasting inner change, we need all the parts of the self to move together.* This is when the self develops organically, without effort.

When stalled, however, the parts of the self start doing something very different (Figure 1.3).

Motivationally, in terms of wants, instead of thinking of what we want as simply adding to our life, such as wanting to be a freelancer in the earlier example, we'd think of it as something that would

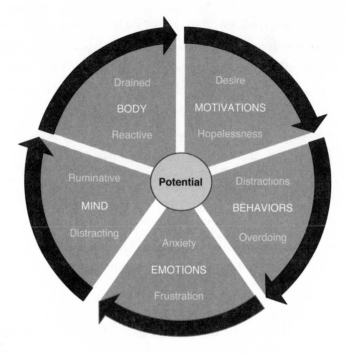

FIGURE 1.3 The Stalled Self

fill a gap in our life. The want may get very intense and may turn into a *desire*—a chronically unfulfilled goal. This kind of desire does not affect only one part of our life but colors its totality in dark hues. Whenever Abhinav's strategies to work less failed, he could no longer fully enjoy other parts of his life, whether family, friends, or recreation. During the little time he did spend with his family or friends, he wasn't able to be fully present. He would drift away mentally, fantasizing about how amazing his life would be if only he could work less. It's as if the one thing that remained unchanged was a dark cloud over the rest of his life.

This intensification of a want into a desire, punctuated by occasional hopelessness, is a natural motivational outcome of chronically unfulfilled wants. When we don't get what we want for a long time, we can lose hope, yet even this hopelessness is temporary since the motivational system evolved to press its claims until fulfilled. We can try to stop wanting some change or pretend to ourselves or others that we no longer want it, but the desire would surge again. The motivational system has evolved to continue pulling us forward, despite our trying to give up.

Behaviorally, desire and hopelessness would lead us to *alternate between overdoing and distractions.* Desire makes us hurry to achieve our goals, and we pour time and energy into self-change. Like a dieter who keeps starting new diets, we would keep overdoing activities that never seem to add up to self-change. At times it would seem we are getting ahead, but these advances would be temporary and opposed by the constant and lurking threat of the relapse into our "old selves." When this happens, overdoing gives way to distractions, where we abandon what we desire and try to forget about it.

Abhinav continually deployed strategies to reduce his work. Sometimes he tried suggestions he read about in books or followed recommendations from friends. He hired coaches, therapists, and other professionals to help with the change. He would throw all his energy behind the endeavor, hoping this would be the time when he would finally make the change. Yet when the strategies failed, he would be overcome by great disappointment and resignation, which led to giving up his efforts and doing other things to forget he gave up. He would continue his old work pattern and, when not working, distract himself with news, social media, or watching TV. But after a while, the unceasing pulse of his desire would activate, and he would start again, his efforts escalating. This rhythm of overdoing and distractions is well known to all of us who have tried to change our behavior, only to have run out of willpower when life's stresses got in the way.

In the **emotional** realm, the long-unfulfilled desire can permeate our life. We would have either a specific *fear of never reaching our goal* or a broader sense of anxiety that would expand to encompass all other activities and goals. It's difficult to relax and do enjoyable things if the looming unsatisfied want is always in the background. Even when Abhinav was spending time at home, playing with his kids, or making dinner with his wife, he was experiencing the background feeling of frustration. After all, he'd think to himself in those moments, if he could solve the problem of working too much, he could have many more enjoyable moments like this and change his life around. Many negative emotions show up when we feel stuck. There could be anger at ourselves and the world for being denied the one thing we want the most. A sense of hopelessness, dread, restlessness, and despair is common. After all, what's the joy in living if the thing we desperately desire is never to be had?

These negative emotions are often fueled by our mind, which spins out beliefs or narratives about what past failures mean. Usually, these include the stories of something being wrong with us such that the fulfillment will always be unreachable; something wrong with other people, who can be seen as the direct obstacles or competitors for the desired thing; or something wrong with the world, which is seen as corrupt or organized in a way to never allow the achievement of the desired thing. Sometimes our mind produces unrealistic fantasies of what fulfillment of our desire would mean. Abhinav would fantasize about how completely transformed all aspects of his life would be if only he could work less.

An additional outcome of repeated failures would be the **mind's** *ruminative or obsessive thinking* about how to gain our goal while increasingly doubting that it is possible. The obsession with the goal would permeate our life to the exclusion of other goals. It would also make it difficult to maintain peace of mind as we make some advances toward the goal. Are we going to lose it? Could it somehow turn out badly? And what is the chance that such success can continue? For example, when Abhinav's attempts at working less worked well for more than a week, his mind would proceed to catastrophic possibilities—what if he declined a patient who would not be able to get care anywhere else and he inadvertently caused this hypothetical person further injury or even death? What if there was a catastrophic economic downturn so that his reduced work would financially devastate his family? Despite occasionally achieving (partially or temporarily) the object of our intense desire, the complete fulfillment and the inner freedom we hope to gain from it would remain elusive.

Another trick that our mind plays on us when we are experiencing action paralysis is to try to mask hopelessness and resignation with the appearance of genuine acceptance. Our inner voice, then, sounds something like this: "I'm fine without it. Maybe this way is better. I'm even better off without it." Yet, despite these thin reassurances and the many distractions we may employ to stop thinking about what we want the most, giving up feels like an impossible option.

Finally, the **body** cannot but be drained by all the mental, emotional, and behavioral activity that keeps leading nowhere. It's easy to forget that the stress of inner conflict is energetically expensive. If ruminative thinking about past failures and future fantasies continues for an extended period, the body under stress may start showing signs of illness (according to psychoneuroimmunology studies).[1]

The body does something else—which holds the key to why the whole Wheel of Self stops turning in the developmental way. In addition to being our active vehicle in the world, the body's job is to hold our learnings in our nervous system and make them available to us as we face increasingly complex situations. The learnings don't need to be conscious. Though sometimes implicit, these invisible beliefs are still active in our lives. *When we are young, emotionally intense threats, losses, and rejections can be "overlearned."* Abhinav's parents, who were immigrants, made many difficult sacrifices so that he and his brother could get the education they did. Abhinav's early experiences affected how he thought of work and sacrifice in his own life, unconsciously pushing him to work more. Memories of his family's struggles and his feelings of sadness, guilt, and fear were still vivid inside him.

Many of us carry such "active" memories in our bodies, whether of our early threats, embarrassments, loneliness, or rejection. Trauma researchers show how the body carries the continued threat of early situations and acts on the present circumstances as if they were the past.[2] This, then, gives us a clue as to why the whole self-system— mind, emotions, body, motivation, and behavior—gets stalled. If the self were, in fact, in danger, it would be rational to hurry, worry, obsess, and get exhausted. The self-system acts rationally but mistakes the present for the past and, in doing so, renders itself ineffective. *The stalled self-system is the self in a cloud of time distortion.* If early overlearned experiences distort how the self interacts with our everyday reality, we are not acting in relation to what is before us but reacting to what is behind us.

Now we have a more detailed picture of what happens to the self when it stalls. Before we find out how to restart each part of the self, it's important to reflect on what parts of our life need further development. This will help us personalize the learnings in Part II and apply them to the very thing we want the most. As we go along, throughout the book, we will follow Abhinav's and others' stories as they start moving their Wheels of Self again.

RED FLAGS OF STAGNATION

How do we know what aspect of our life would benefit from development? It would be something without which we feel our life would not be fulfilled, something we have been trying to gain repeatedly without success, something that makes us worried, frustrated, obsessed, frantic, hopeless, and finally, exhausted. We may spend many months ignoring it, yet it never really leaves the background of our consciousness. If this description doesn't bring anything to your mind, here are four other cues that could alert you to your stalled "wheels."

Behind schedule. Having strong wants frequently leads to a continual comparison with others. If we are unfulfilled in a particular domain (finances, relationships, fitness, creativity, etc.), we are likely to be inquisitive about other people's achievements in that same domain. Often this leads to self-torment when we compare ourselves to those who have done better than us or glimmers of hope when we find people who were "late starters" like us but still managed to make it. This is the feeling of being "behind schedule," missing a crucial opportunity, the feeling that "the ship has sailed," or "what's the point of starting now," while at the same time being unable to stop wanting the very thing we are so "behind" in. We may feel other people have built better careers, families, bodies, friendships, or skills and that, by this age (no matter what that age may be), we should have achieved more or be more fulfilled in our life. Notice that this feeling of being "behind" is entirely age-independent, so 20-year-olds are as likely to suffer from it as 70-year-olds.

Envy. A related but different experience is envy. A person with an intense desire for something will frequently be around people for whom the thing that they want badly comes naturally and without any effort. For example, let's say that no matter how much money we make, we find it difficult to get out of "the red"—but we know dozens of people who make less than we do, have an excellent standard of living, and are somehow always in "the black." Even more maddeningly, we may know people who, once they decide they need more money, are showered with opportunities and cash. Or maybe we have been trying to have a meaningful relationship for years, and yet our love life is a series of relational shipwrecks, while our child-hood friend has found the love of her life at 20 and is giddily happy 15 years into her marriage. Most people ascribe this to luck, "dumb" luck in particular, to highlight the undeserved nature of the riches showered upon their fortunate friends and acquaintances and to defend against the thought that luck may have nothing to do with it.

Although somewhat unpleasant to think about, wanting what other people have while at the same time being irritated that they have it can be a great clue that our development has stalled in that domain of our life. Envy implies more than comparing our life to that of another person or even wanting to have something similar. It means we wouldn't mind seeing them fail, and if this were to happen, we may feel schadenfreude, taking some pleasure in the misfortunes of others. When envious, we may discuss information about unfor-tunate events in other people's lives (a career failure, a divorce, or a loss of their investments in a dubious scheme) eagerly and with gusto. This makes sense psychologically: if we believe we can't have what we badly want, it is comforting to know other people can't have it either.

While most of us shrink away from awareness that we are envi-ous, facing and hearing our envy can be a great boon to self-development. Envy highlights the parts of our life in which we feel unfulfilled and underdeveloped, and if we were to take its clue, we could begin the hard work of restarting our growth.

Advice that never works. You have probably at least once been in the shoes of either the giver or seeker of advice that doesn't work. In one scenario, a person to whom something comes naturally gives (either unsolicited or solicited) advice to someone who desires that same thing intensely. Imagine a frugal person giving financial advice to a spendthrift. Despite goodwill and the best effort of all the parties involved, such advice leads nowhere. It is either not executed or is executed in a way that mysteriously doesn't produce any of the outcomes that the advice giver was hoping to produce.

This makes sense since advice given with the best intentions by someone naturally good at something is then interpreted by the distorted lens of the person who is terrible at it. If we receive such advice while "stuck" in some part of our development, we may discard it for various seemingly logical but self-deceptive reasons, postpone its implementation until the "right" time, or follow it too literally or too vaguely for it to have any practical impact. Ultimately, both the advice giver and seeker will likely end up frustrated and disappointed. We may want to reflect on what advice we seek most, what is on our self-help or inspirational bookshelf, and what workshops we have spent the most money on—this reflection may guide us to know which domains in ourselves are still to be fulfilled.

Being immature. It's one of the self's mysteries how the development in one aspect of self may cease while the development in other domains of our lives continues naturally. This is how we may end up being a perfectly competent 53-year-old professional with great friends and finances who, when romantically rejected, behaves as a petulant 16-year-old and, when abandoned, withdraws as a scared 7-year-old. This fact, that adults occasionally behave as if they were chronologically younger or immature, is frequently pointed out when it happens to others. Yet when we notice an immature outburst in ourselves, we often give ourselves excuses—we were tired, upset, or it was someone else's fault. Very few of us are willing to give the immature parts of ourselves a closer look. And for a good reason. These aspects of us, stuck on the way to development, represent the most painfully unmet wants that have been continually denied and sometimes temporarily abandoned. Yet in that very same place lies, of course, the greatest potential of fulfillment.

OUTER BLOCKS TO CHANGE

There is one more thing we need to consider before we begin our process of inner change. In our attempts to become more fulfilled, we may underestimate how our social world may react to our change. Other people are potent causal forces in our world, and this is seen clearly when our inner change causes disruptions and complications in social relationships.

When people enter relationships of any kind (and become colleagues, acquaintances, friends, lovers, partners), there is usually an implicit social contract that is drawn between them—and that is that both people will keep "being themselves." That usually means that many values, emotional patterns, behaviors, and beliefs will stay recognizably similar over time. This stability people exhibit over time makes others believe that each of us has an unchanging personality. It makes us think we know others well.

Why is this kind of "knowing" important to us? Because it makes us believe that it will keep the other person predictable in relation to whatever social contract we have entered. There is comfort in knowing that Friend A will always help us move, Friend B will come over and comfort us when we are sad, and Friend C can be counted on only when having fun. What happens if Friend A suddenly says he has no time and Friend B starts asking unsettling questions rather than comforting us? We would think they are behaving "out of character." If this behavior were to continue, we could decide that we don't know who they are anymore, grow apart, or even end the relationship. Other people's change is unsettling because it leaves us to the vulnerability that they may change in a way that does not suit us, for which we are not prepared, and that we do not like.

What would a healthy approach to others' continuing development be? It would be like the attitude of healthy parents: they know their children are growing and take for granted that their relationship will have to continually change to be able to keep up with the child's development. This is the case no matter how threatening these changes may be. As adults, we can do the same for each other—we can see our partner's, friends', and colleagues' development as an exciting opportunity to learn to support, encourage, and adapt our relationships to that change, no matter how much we may like the comfort of the status quo.

Occasionally we may develop in ways that make it difficult to maintain our relationships in the ways we are accustomed to. A couple in which one person has discovered the joys of "living in the moment" while the other is concerned with long-term security may need to separate their financial accounts for the sake of relational peace. A partner of someone who has become a fitness buff and wants to spend a lot of time doing physical activities may have to spend more time alone or with friends. Developmental change challenges relationships.

The other option is to forfeit our own development, and that of the other person, so that we can keep the relationship in its original state. It's like saying, "If you stay in your box, I'll stay in mine." So, as you decide whether to begin your own process of change, keep in mind that those around you may be startled, and even made uncomfortable, by your "new self." Given that we know how challenging this can be, we can communicate every step of the way, to give the best chance to the evolving relationships.

Just as we prefer others to be predictable, we like to know who we are. Studies have shown that people seek out self-verifying information, engaging with others in a way that will confirm what they already believe to be true about themselves.[3] This perception of permanent personality—unchanging stability in who we are—can be a serious obstacle to development. *Who we believe we are is often an enemy of who we want to become.* As humans, we are fond of categorizations—whether we are put into a box by a personality test, a horoscope, or a leadership questionnaire. Being told that we are an "introvert" or a "Pisces" or a "driver" may be thought-provoking as long as it doesn't entrench us in a glass box that development is supposed to shatter. If we think of personality as early learned skills, then our development lies on the opposite pole of our trait "box." If chronically extroverted, we may need to learn to be fulfilled in our own company; if too amiable, we may need to learn assertiveness; if too assertive, amiability.

Though we may like our "boxes," or even prefer the status quo, the perception of there being no movement in self is illusory. Our potential will keep pulling us forward; if we prefer not to move, we have to exert force in the opposite direction. What looks like stability is a vibrating tension between our fears of change and developmental potential pulling in opposite directions. Despite its appearance, the status quo, when applied to personal development, is not static, not peaceful, and can rapidly yield to either fear or development, at any moment.

HOW TO USE THIS BOOK

You can use this book in two ways: (1) as a manual about what self is and how it develops and (2) as a guide to your own development.

If you focus on the first objective, the book may provide you insights into how different parts of the self operate, why self-development stalls, and what it would take to create sustained self-change. Ideally, you would also be able to parse better the widely varying psychological writings you are likely to see in scientific and pop literature. The hope is that you will gain enough insight and expertise to know what of the myriad psychological advice you are bombarded with daily is likely to work, under what conditions, and to what effect.

Another way to read this book is not just as a curious student of human nature but as someone who wants to make meaningful changes in your own life. If so, you can use this book to catalyze your natural growth. You can read it and do the exercises at your own pace. Please use them as guides to exploration, not as mandatory homework or a painful chore. You can experiment with the techniques, devise new ones based on the principles you learn, and do whatever you feel works for you while trying to catalyze your own developmental process. There are as many routes to development as there are people. It's important you follow your own way.

Like all living things, the human organism has evolved to keep trying to develop as long as it lives. That means that even when the development slows or stalls, such as when we observe a plant not given enough sun or water, the developmental process doesn't die away until the organism dies. As long as we are alive something in us will continually try to pull us forward and propel us to grow. Unlike plants or animals who are forced to react to their environment as they find it, we are fortunate to use our formidable consciousness to make the inner changes required to rearrange our outer lives for the benefit of our growth.

Learning about how the self works and how to facilitate its development takes time, energy, and the belief we have the inner wisdom that will help us fulfill parts of ourselves that have never or rarely experienced fulfillment. It's possible, but it's work. You may want to read the book but not do the work quite yet, and that is understandable. Change in some domain of self, even a positive one, changes your whole life, and only you can know when you are ready.

PART II

WORKING WITH THE WHEEL

CHAPTER TWO

MOTIVATION

What are **wants**? They are the force of our **motivational system**, pulling us toward our **potential**. *All wants are developmental at source*, there to guide us toward growth. Although plants and animals also have potential (as they are alive), they don't need wants since they act out their development spontaneously. Given enough air, water, and soil, a flower doesn't need to be "pulled" toward growth—it just grows. Furthermore, plants and animals don't have a choice in their development, whereas humans do. A dog given a treat is not likely to experience it as a choice, whereas if we want a pizza, we can decide whether to have it or not.

Another way that we are different from our animal and plant cousins is that while their potential (Darwinian survival and reproduction) is the same for all members of the species, humans are born with a *unique and expanded range of potentials*. We have emotional, relational, intellectual, creative, aesthetic, and spiritual potentials, to mention just a few, and they are different for each person. So, while all fig trees are moving toward their single potential of growing, bearing figs, and reproducing to make more fig trees, each of us has a unique set of potentials, like a fingerprint, which makes it impossible to guess our destination ahead of time. While parents dream of what their children may become, it is the children themselves who carry the secret of their own potential.

Let me now introduce Kai, a software developer in his late 20s who had struggled with weight since childhood. When Kai was young, his mother and father had very different approaches to his weight. His mother cooked his favorite meals and gave him his favorite snacks to calm him down when he was upset. Kai's father tried to control what he ate and would wake him up early in the morning and force him to exercise. Kai had been on different diets and exercise regimes most of his life. He tried paleo, keto, low-carb, and low-fat diets, as well as fasting, and while he had some temporary successes, he would inevitably break his diets in times of high stress. The same happened with exercise routines. He tried spinning, running, fast walking, Pilates, strength training, and had even hired a personal trainer. Inevitably, within months, he would start missing his sessions. A training session missed because of a work trip or one of his parents' health emergencies would turn into two or three, at which point Kai would decide to restart later when he had more time and was less stressed.

Kai's initial response to the first two assumptions about motivation—that all wants are developmental at source and that each human has a set of unique potentials—was to challenge them. He made two interesting points. If all wants were developmental at source, what about destructive wants—for example, wanting to sit on the couch eating chips and ice cream while watching TV? How about a want to destroy other species for a bit of extra profit, a want to protect one's privilege at the expense of countless others, or a want for power that destroys innumerable lives? Kai couldn't connect how his late-night cravings for junk food or wanting to not move from his chair for many hours were "developmental at the source." His experience of wants was that most of what he really wanted was bad, and his job was to fight these wants and replace them with healthy behaviors, such as eating foods outlined by his nutritionist and doing exercises assigned by his trainer.

Kai's second point was that since he couldn't trust which of his wants were developmental and which were destructive, it was impossible to use them as a link to his potential. He felt his wants were not trustworthy guides to his development, and it was confusing and stressful even to think of them. He was starting to believe that the best path forward was to study what potential looked like for successful people and to strive for that himself.

What Kai would soon learn was how to read each of his destructive wants to reach their developmental core and, with time, relearn to trust his core wants. But before that was possible, he had to understand (1) how wants work and (2) how they transform from developmental to destructive.

SEARCHING FOR OUR CORE WANTS

Wants rarely enter our consciousness in their pure form. Instead, they come into our minds as associations. You could think, "I am thirsty," but more likely you'll think, "I want water or coffee or soda." Why? Because ever since we started having wants during childhood, they have been satisfied in particular ways, and the associations we have built around them have become invisible. You may want bread with butter and jam in the morning but may not remember when or why it was that you first started associating breakfast with that combination of foods. Your mother may still tell stories about how at two years of age, you didn't want to go to sleep without a pink, fuzzy blanket, but even she will probably not be able to pinpoint the moment you associated that blanket with feeling safe.

As we grow up and start wanting more complex things, like friends, careers, and relationships, these sets of associations become more complex and invisible. In addition to experiencing our wants, our young minds must navigate a field of narratives (from parents, siblings, schoolmates, teachers) about which wants are proper to have and also the preferable means of fulfilling them. Most kids who ask for ice cream for breakfast get a quick lesson from their parents on what is appropriate food to want first thing in the morning.

One way to think of how wants function is to start with **the core, or developmental, wants** and place them at the center of a set of increasingly widening circles. Let's place a want for social connection or friendships at the center of the circle (Figure 2.1). We could also think about it in the opposite direction: that is, not wanting to feel isolated and lonely. This want needs a method of fulfillment. Depending on which culture, family, peer group, school, religion, or continent we are thrown into by the accident of our birth, we will start constructing beliefs and narratives of how to achieve what we want. (Another term for **beliefs** is "**constructs**"—it highlights that they are constructed over time, even before we understand language, and can stay implicit throughout adulthood.)

In the first example (on the far left), we may intuitively learn that the way to get close friendships is to treat others well so that they feel good being around us. A toddler in a kindergarten may internalize this belief or construct just by trial and error while interacting

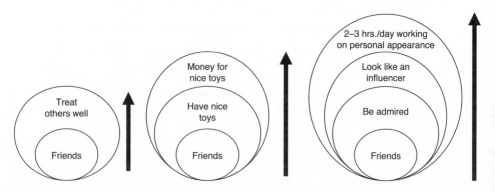

FIGURE 2.1 Layers of Wants

with other toddlers. They will internalize that hitting, biting, and pushing other toddlers will result in no one wanting to play with them, while being friendly, caring, and sharing will bring other toddlers closer. This internalized construct is implicit and can be built without language being used. In the case of the toddler, the want is fulfilled directly. Notice that *a want plus an efficient construct or belief will result in direct fulfillment of the want*. As we grow up, we update this construct to be age-appropriate and use it to build other friendships.

But what happens if, for whatever reason, we miss this lesson and have difficulties making friends? The want will still be active and we'll be searching for other constructs to help fulfill it. As we grow up and gain language, our constructs are shaped not only by trial and error but the beliefs of those around us too.

Let's say we started elementary school and are still struggling to make friends. Our uncle, wishing to help, gives us advice that we can make friends by having nice toys (which others will desire, so they'll want to be close to us). Notice that *a want plus an inefficient construct or belief will spark another layer of want* (another circle). Observe the middle circles of Figure 2.1. Wanting to have nice stuff could, in turn, spark another want—for money. This belief may persist well into adulthood. While the nature of the toys may change (into yachts, luxury cars, or fancy watches), the belief that having expensive things will somehow produce friendships may remain.

Let's move on to the third set of circles in Figure 2.1. Imagine we are already in high school, still feeling isolated and lonely. We may notice that kids who look like social media influencers tend to have a whole clique of other kids around them, admiring them and wanting to be a part of their circle. Desiring to make friends, we may start believing that if we could look more like influencers, others would be drawn to us. Notice again that a want plus an inefficient construct will spark another layer of want. Still being unfulfilled, wanting to look like influencers may make us want to spend hours worrying about our personal appearance. We would buy the products the influencers recommend, diet, or spend hours in the gym. The energy with which we would pursue the products, gym, and dieting is really the energy of wanting friends misguided by false constructs.

What makes a construct or belief effective? They need to "work"—that is, have a high likelihood of leading to the fulfillment of the want. The most effective constructs tend to relate thematically to the want itself. Treating others well is relational in nature and much more likely to lead to close friendships than would having an interesting job or looking like an influencer (which are neither necessary nor sufficient for building a close friendship). Furthermore, the effective construct will be something *a person can do themselves, accessible directly, producing a one-layer fulfillment of the want.* For example, a one-layer construct for wanting to be creative in writing would be to begin small creative projects and learn about the craft (reading a lot, writing short stories and poems, etc.) right away. A non-efficient construct would be waiting to enroll in an MFA in creative writing program to begin writing. Notice that nothing stops us (and we may well benefit) from further education, but the *want itself requires direct action now and not in the future.*

Ineffective constructs promise fulfillment in the far future and cause the core wants to get associated with other wants, which then spin further ones, each increasingly more distant from the original want. The energy that animates the entire set of circles is the core developmental want at the center. In the example in Figure 2.1, we will continue spinning out wants prompted by the central, or core, want for having friendships. The further we get from the center, the less satisfied we feel when we achieve the outer-layer want, since it only peripherally (if at all) satisfies the want at the center. For example, spending hours at the gym or in online communities surrounding influencers may give us some sense of community with others with similar interests. However, since we still lack the skills to build deeper and more lasting friendships, we are not likely to be able to meet our core want fully.

The key to our development and fulfillment, then, is to try to excavate and satisfy our core wants directly.

Success without Fulfillment

The paradox of success without fulfillment, where we feel dissatisfied and restless despite having accomplished societally admired heights of achievement, is often based on the distance between our core wants and the outer layer of wants we have achieved. The further we are from the core, the less satisfied we will likely be. Let's say we want self-respect. Buying an expensive watch (an outer-layer want) because we want admiration (middle layer), which we think will give us self-respect (core want), is not likely to work very well or for long. On the other hand, knowing ourselves and acting in accordance with who we are will directly produce the self-respect we want.

We also often forget that experience of fulfillment is process-based rather than outcome-based. For example, our want for friendships is fulfilled by *engaging in* friendships, not by knowing that we *"have"* friends. The fulfillment of creative wants is satisfied in the *process of writing* (or cooking, gardening, building, etc.) rather than in *having* a story published or finishing a garden. If we see fulfillment as an outcome rather than a process, we will strive for goals that are supposed to lead us (indirectly) to it without ever seeming to get there. We may get the outcome but not the fulfillment.

Let's turn our attention to Emily. Emily grew up as the oldest child in a well-off family of bankers. Her father, a hedge fund manager, made sure she went to the best schools, hoping his daughter would follow him in the profession. Emily loved to draw; a passion encouraged by a high school teacher who had observed a talent in young Emily rarely seen in her classroom. When Emily approached her father to discuss her hope that she would go to art school, she wasn't rebuffed. Her father was understanding, even supportive, of her passion. He reminded Emily that he loved music as a young man (he had played violin and even kept one in his office) and understood her feelings. He explained that if she was serious about pursuing a career in arts, she would need some way to support herself financially. One way to do it would be to give music lessons or find small side jobs. Another way would be to study finance, make a lot of money quickly, and then dedicate as much time to her art as she wanted. This is precisely the option that Emily's grandfather presented to her father when he tried to become a violinist. It shaped Emily's constructs in the following way (Figure 2.2).

Freedom to create was associated with having enough money to retire early, which in turn sparked the want to become a banker, which then activated a further want to ensure her investments were performing well.

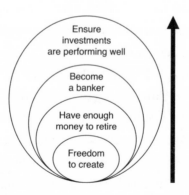

FIGURE 2.2 Emily's Layers of Wants

When I met Emily in one of the Executive MBA classes, she was already a highly successful wealth management professional in her late 40s. She had a real estate portfolio her peers were envious of and had already reached highs of achievement that surpassed even her father's expectations. She also had good relationships—with her spouse, family, and a group of supportive friends. Emily noticed, though, that she was often restless, dissatisfied, or agitated without reason. She spent every free moment monitoring the performance of her investments, which would calm her for a time. She felt like she wanted more money despite a feeling that, deep inside, she was not a greedy person. She wanted to know what, finally, would make her feel satisfied.

To understand that, Emily had to turn the arrow back down, starting on the outer layer (wanting more money) and then exploring downward, looking for the core want (using Technique 1, which we will cover at the end of the chapter). When she finally understood that her obsession with money was driven by wanting freedom to create, she had two questions: (1) What's the point of knowing this now, given she could not become the artist she wanted to be as a young woman? And (2) did this mean that, in order to be fulfilled, she had to give up her career and the lifestyle to which she was accustomed?

Both questions betrayed that Emily still thought of fulfillment as an outcome rather than a process. In reality, she could *start to create* that very day. Her creative want would then begin to be fulfilled no matter whether she became a famous artist or not, or whether she continued or abandoned her wealthy lifestyle. What Emily had forgotten is that freedom to create was different from "becoming an artist." As long as she could find an extra 15 minutes in the day and some art supplies, it was always available to her. It is *creating* that would engage the *process* of *fulfilling the want*.

Emily's questions and hesitation make sense. If we have lived most of our lives assuming that our fulfillment is supposed to come later, after some outcome has been achieved, it would be scary to realize that the possibility of fulfillment was there all along and continues to be there now, each moment of the day. Sometimes, in order to not regret the fulfillment we could have had in the past, we forfeit the fulfillment we can have now and in the future.

Other Complications

As we go along in life, some (or almost all) of this lattice of associations sparked by the core wants becomes invisible to us. We know what we want for that moment and build goals for the future based on life outcomes we wish for ourselves (often in the hope they will fulfill us). We can think of goals as entirely verbal and elaborate constructs about how to reach a particular outcome. For example, we may want a romantic connection in our life and set goals that are likely to get us there directly (going on dates) or not (trying to get a perfect body).

The difference between a want and a goal is that a want is a motivational force, whereas a goal is a story about how to reach a specific outcome in our life. Most of us set goals in the hope of being fulfilled by them, but that's not always necessary. We may have a goal of doing a course that will improve our chances of promotion at work, even if we don't enjoy the course and know that the new job won't bring us fulfillment.

We seem not very accurate when anticipating what will make us fulfilled. Despite the fact that, for example, people living in colder regions of the United States expect Californians to be happier due to sunnier and warmer weather, research shows that they are not.[1] Most people think winning the lottery would make them ecstatically happy, but according to a study, a year after a great win, the winners are no happier than those in the control group who did not win a lottery.[2]

Having shorter-term goals that build into longer-term ones is more likely to allow us to evaluate if we are mistaken about what will make us fulfilled. Instead of moving to California, we could visit for a few months and see if we feel more satisfied there. If we want to become physicians, we can audit anatomy and biochemistry classes to see if we enjoy what we learn; we can shadow a physician sitting in her office all day, seeing patients. What we want to avoid is thinking that the achievement of a long-term goal will necessarily bring us fulfillment. *Wants are fulfilled only in the present, not in the future.*

The opposite is also true. Sometimes, in a lucky turn of events, we do something we'd never thought we wanted (a boring job, for example) and end up being much more fulfilled than we anticipated because it satisfies some want at the very center (like having comradeship or belonging to a community) of which we were not even aware. Unfortunately, the alternative is more common. When we are disappointed with how we feel once we reach a particular goal, we don't stop to reflect and reassess. Instead, we keep moving outward, spinning out more circles of want.

Aggravating the problem of not accurately predicting what will fulfill us is social pressure around wants. We may be taught (or learn by observation) that our wants are not legitimate. We may be told we are not supposed to want to work in arts (instead of business), not supposed to dedicate ourselves to a career (instead of family), or not supposed to love someone because of their race, religion, or gender. Indeed, much unsolicited advice is given about what people *should* want. No matter which wants truly animate us, the world will try to add to them, modify them, and sometimes replace them with others. *Our ability to fulfill our potential depends on holding on to the invisible thread that connects us to our wants.*

It is also easy to moralize about wants in the usual way: to imply material wants are always shallow while relational wants are always profound. There are many material wants (like nurturing one's body or having a beautiful home) that can fulfill deep developmental wants (for health or beauty, for example). Only when material wants are used instrumentally as a stepping stone to other wants (such as status, respect, or relationships) do they mislead and so trap us. The same is true for engaging in relationships purely as a stepping stone for achieving professional advancement (which is the dark side of "networking"). Another example of this is ensuring we have a nice-looking family because it goes well with our aspirations as a political candidate.

The way to find our path back to core wants is to understand how wants, despite their developmental origin, can become distorted and destructive. Up to this point, we learned that core wants can build layers that are entirely unrelated to developmental wants and won't fulfill them. But how do we end up with **destructive** wants?

DESTRUCTIVE WANTS

At this point, we need to understand how it is that **destructive** wants—wanting to undermine, hurt, or destroy oneself and others—start with a developmental want at the very center. Let's begin with a basic want to feel safe and protected. Imagine we were taught as a child that the only way to feel safe in the world is if we show everyone (verbally or physically) that we are stronger than they are. In a classroom or a workplace, this could make us into a bully. Or imagine we were taught that the only way to feel protected is to make sure that a group we belong to (racial, ethnic, gender, etc.) is superior to other groups (Figure 2.3). If this construct is accepted and acted on, what soon follows is wanting to diminish (and, in extreme cases, destroy) other groups that are seen as competitors or threats. Depending on the constructs we have been

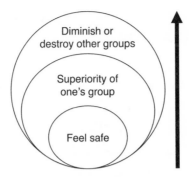

FIGURE 2.3 From Developmental to Destructive Wants

taught about how to achieve safety or worth, the number of steps to destructive wants that bring about hurtful speech and action may be very small.

The destructive wants lay at the farthest edges of what, at the core, are developmental wants, such as to feel safe, attended to, worthy, or loved. So, whether we send a small hurtful comment toward our partner or anonymously post a hate-filled tirade against immigrants, at the center of these actions are largely unfulfilled wants. A person whose core want for self-respect is not fulfilled may try to bring it about by terrorizing his employees or children in the hope their fear will somehow turn into respect.

The destructive wants come into being through moving away from realistic and healthy constructs of how to satisfy basic developmental wants. For this reason, the rhetoric of "good" and "bad" people, with many of us thinking of ourselves as good and other people as bad, further feeds the destructiveness we often see around us. Understanding how destructive wants come about helps us understand that if we don't fulfill our core wants, we, too, may become a destructive force to ourselves and others.

Giving the same weight to developmental and destructive impulses (rather than seeing a path from one to the other) also alienates us from our desires. When Kai thought of his want for junk food simply as "bad," he felt there were parts of him that he needed to suppress or shut down. Rather than get away from his destructive wants, he needed to get closer to them (analytically) to understand what core developmental want energized his self-destructive behaviors and needed to be satisfied directly.

The first challenge to regaining trust in our wants is learning to see through these chains of associations. While we now understand why we want to hurt or destroy *others*, we return to Kai's question— how did he develop wants that ended up hurting *him*? After all, it is difficult to have trust in our wants if we keep wanting unhealthy snacks, destructive relationships, or at the extreme end, develop addictions to prescription drugs, gambling, or sex. What kind of association errors get us to self-destructiveness? We can think of these misguided associations as two types of detours our wants make on the way to satisfaction: physiological and psychological.

Physiological Detours

The feeling of comfort that we get from being nurtured through food or being relieved of physical pain is so potent in the human psyche that it can be counted on to make us feel good even when we encounter unrelated problems—loneliness, professional stagnation, interpersonal conflict. Regarding food, we have evolved to like and feel pleasure when tasting sweet and fatty foods, which is no big surprise given that the *Homo* species have been hunters and foragers for at least a few million years. If you have ever spent time with a toddler on the verge of a tantrum, you will have learned that sometimes the quickest way to end the crisis is to offer them something sweet and fatty, such as ice cream. The physiological comfort of ice cream can soothe the emotional or relational pain the child feels, and this fact can be learned early on in childhood. This is why children whose parents comfort them emotionally through food become adults who comfort themselves with food and subsequently suffer health consequences.[3]

Kai's mother had done precisely that—gave him his favorite snacks when he was upset so that he associated sweet and fatty foods with not feeling distressed or lonely early in his childhood. Whereas wants build from the center outward, to understand them, we start with the outer-layer want and try to find our way to the center. For Kai, it looked like this (Figure 2.4). He started with the outward layer, wanting to eat unhealthy foods, and realized it gave him a feeling of being comforted and loved.

The problem with the physiological comfort that food brings is that it makes us feel good while it does not necessarily address the want that activated the eating behavior—such as loneliness, anxiety, or other psychological pain. This becomes rather obvious in adulthood.

For example, if someone breaks up with us and we are dealing with the anguish of rejection, we may head to the store to buy a tub of ice cream and, when back home, proceed to eat the whole thing. Notice that our want at that moment is relational. We may want to have the relationship miraculously repair itself and to have the person back. Short of that, we may want the comfort of a relational kind, perhaps to call a friend, have them talk to us, or give us a hug. This is the comfort most closely related, psychologically, to the issue at

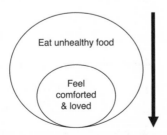

FIGURE 2.4   Kai's Exploration of Destructive Wants

hand. But perhaps it's late in the night, and our friend works in the morning. Or maybe we haven't been in touch recently and now feel embarrassed to call asking for support. Whatever the case may be, it is far less complicated to head to a store for ice cream. The ice cream doesn't satisfy the relational need, which is why no matter how large the tub, we may keep eating until it's done. But it can be bought in the middle of the night, and everyone can still make it to work the next morning without the pains and exertions of maintaining friendships or the feeling of vulnerability when asking for help.

This substitutive ability (such as consuming food to reduce loneliness) is perhaps most dangerous in relation to the physiological overlap between physical and social pain systems.[4] *Social* rejection (such as being socially excluded) activates neural circuits involved in *physical* pain.[5] This means that there is a shared underlying circuitry for pain that gets activated whether we break an arm or have our heart broken by a lover. Researchers have found that over-the-counter pain medications, such as acetaminophen, can reduce *social* pain[6] and influence how people experience social distress.[7]

Let's say we need to go to a hospital for back surgery. In addition to the back injury, we are also dealing with a lot of stress at work and feelings of isolation and loneliness. Once in the hospital, we are given painkillers to manage our pain during post-op recovery. Most of us would be unaware that, in addition to reducing physical pain, the drug was also making us feel less lonely or upset. We would only notice that once we are released from the hospital and no longer on painkillers, we may feel *more* upset or lonely. The intensity of our want to keep taking the drugs even without having physical pain would depend on the intensity of our psychological pain and, therefore, how comforting the painkiller felt. *The more psychological pain and unfulfilled wants we have, the more vulnerable we will be to physical and behavioral addictions.*

Most of us have learned a few paths to feel good in our lives. It could be anything—food, pills, alcohol, watching TV, or even seemingly very productive behaviors, such as working hard, exercising, or socializing with friends. Yet whenever we use our comfort "thing" to reduce the emotional signal of discomfort that is *unrelated* to it, we may miss the opportunity to satisfy the want that is signaling a need for fulfillment. If we are lonely and have no friends, hard work, pills, or TV won't help; if our work has become no longer stimulating, exercise or spending time with friends won't help. Of course, there are better and worse ways to distract ourselves from having to face and fulfill our wants. Addiction to TV is not as destructive as addiction to meth. But the principle that underlies them both is the same. Whatever things we use to relieve the discomfort of thematically unrelated problems become accomplices to further psychological pain.

We face additional challenges from advertisers who seem to understand this process of substitution far better than most of us. For example, junk food and pornography share an important characteristic. They have been created by commercializing the idea of "super-stimuli." These are human-made creations that exaggerate an aspect (size, color, taste, etc.) of something found in nature. Think of a small bird egg, and then imagine making a fake egg that looks just like it but is the size of an American football. That's exactly what two Nobel-prize-winning scientists (Konrad Lorenz and Nico Tinbergen) did when studying Greylag geese. They found that when a giant egg is positioned close to the real egg, the goose would ignore her own egg and fruitlessly repeat the motion of trying to push the fake egg into the nest.[8] Because the "super-stimulus" triggered an automatic response, the goose was unable to stop pushing the giant egg to the point of exhaustion, completely neglecting her natural eggs.

Similarly, junk food and pornography both cause automatic responses to super-stimuli. Most junk food relies on exaggerated amounts of fat, sugar, and salt, while most pornography combines exaggerated curves, easy sexual availability, and easy partner satisfiability (which is why the human soundtrack to pornography is so loud). In short, these products are created as super-stimuli to activate the automatic action of the human autonomic system. Over time, habituation demands that someone fed on a diet of super-stimuli junk food or pornography will no longer be satisfied with everyday food or their real sexual partners. The whole process wanders impossibly far from the original wants—nurturing the body through food or having a fulfilling sexual interaction with another person.

It seems, then, that our nervous system makes us vulnerable: both by a neural overlap between psychological and physical pain and through reactivity to super-stimuli. These vulnerabilities steer us away from our core wants.

Psychological Detours

It is not only biology that can spawn an endless web of associated wants; it is our own experience that continues to do so throughout our lives. For example, if a person wanted to become a pop musician, and most pop musicians they have seen wore a particular type of clothes and body art, they would naturally associate it with their future musical career. Of course, we all know that just getting fashionable clothes and tattoos will not make us pop artists any more than going to Cuba to write will make us Ernest Hemingway. Or do we?

Let's reflect on how many books are sold about the lives of famous writers or CEOs, the kinds of books hopeful writers and aspiring MBAs pore over for all the juicy details. The well-meaning belief of many successful people is that they have found *the* way to success, and they want to give back wisdom to the people by sharing their path. On our end, we study their habits, clothes, beliefs, waking and sleeping routines, tattoos—and if we turn out not to be successful, we blame ourselves for not being able to stick to other people's routines.

Enter advertisers. As with biological needs, they exploit the substitutive quality of our associations. An athlete, singer, or actor admired by many can become a vehicle to sell perfumes, dresses, belts, shoes, makeup, anti-aging creams, and so forth. It's the associative beauty, riches, fame, and glamour we try to buy. The other strategy is to hitch the product to a want that most people have—such as to have friends, romantic relationships with those seen as beautiful, or even to be beautiful ourselves. A lonely person watching a commercial for beer in which they see a group of beautiful friends laughing and frolicking on the beach may be activated to buy the beer by an associative want for friends and relationships.

Advertisers research the unfilled desires of all different age groups and craft their products accordingly. For example, middle-aged people often suffer under the pressure of difficult marriages, the mess of growing children, and the stress of stalled or ever-expanding careers. Advertisers understand they may want to feel free and unburdened from the complexities of life, so they produce this kind of ad: A handsome, beautifully dressed, man is driving a luxurious car down an empty highway cut into the mountain overlooking a glittering blue ocean. There is no person in sight. There are also no dishes, no dirty diapers, no arguments, no answering emails at midnight. We want to buy simplicity and freedom of his life, but we'll settle for the car.

Should we not find our wants and desires highly suspect, given just how vulnerable we are to being misled?

Reading Our Wants

Given all this—that our wants often have only a peripheral relation to what would develop us and make us feel fulfilled—we could ask whether it is even worthwhile bothering with them. Shouldn't we rather choose from a menu of wants that respectable and admired people have picked for themselves?

As we grow, many of us learn to distrust and distance ourselves from something that, as children, we have little trouble with—knowing what we want. Yet no matter how misguided and manipulated our wants may be, no matter how many misleading layers they spin out, they are the *only* clues we have about where our development and fulfillment lie.

This does not mean that we should act on *all* our wants—since the wants in the outer layers of the circles may lead us away rather than toward the fulfillment of our core wants. They may make us waste many years of our lives, only to realize the achievement we labored for with such intensity does not really fulfill us. Instead, we can **read them**, like we would tracks in the snow, until we find the ones that are close enough to the core want that they seem worth our time and energy. Reading the wants means trying to understand what constructs we used to build outer layers, how connected they really are to the core desires, and what needs to be revised, elaborated, rewritten, or even removed from our circles of wants.

FINDING OUR CENTER

Before describing a step-by-step technique that will guide you as you try to identify your chronically unfulfilled core wants, here are some patterns we will observe once we begin analyzing them.

One solution to all life problems. Sometimes a want at the outermost layer, like going to the gym daily, has many different core wants at the center—which should belong to different circles. Observe Figure 2.5. We may want to go to the gym because it will make us feel healthy and vital (which would be a one-layer want), but more

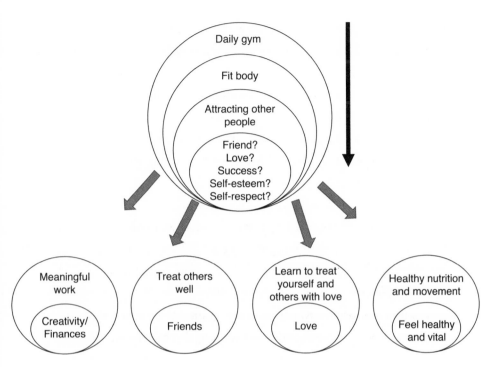

FIGURE 2.5 From One "Outer Layer" to Many Core Wants

often we want it because it will make us feel attractive to others, which we believe will get us friends, lovers, business opportunities, and self-respect.

The same goes for a successful career. A person may think that having professional success is a route to fulfilling all their wants: financial success (and therefore security or freedom), access to attractive partners, interesting friends, approval and love of parents, and the like. Of course, while a career may affect these wants, the only domain that will be continually *fulfilled* by a successful career is the creative/financial one.

Instead of having one set of many-layered circles, with multiple core wants at the center, we need to aim at having multiple small circles. Each small circle would have one layer, thematically related to our core wants. Observe the smaller circles in Figure 2.5. If the core want is relational, the layer needs to be relational; if the core want is physical, the layer needs to be physical.

When Kai, who has struggled throughout his life with food and exercise, explored his wants circles, as seen in Figure 2.6, he found something interesting. When asked what he wanted, he said he wanted to eat healthily. When he worked down from the outer circle toward the core desire, he found out that the reason for wanting to eat healthily was to become fit, to avoid humiliation and a feeling of worthlessness, and therefore feel worthy, successful, and loved. His core wants were entirely unrelated to the body. To move forward with his stated wants, he needed to address the core wants he identified in addition to tackling the issue of the body.

Strong "opposing" wants. When it comes to chronically unfulfilled wants, we can suspect that we want to do the opposite of what we claim we want. We may want to finish our homework and want to procrastinate. We may want to stop smoking and keep smoking. We want to eat healthy food and want to eat junk food. Given that the opposing want is also something we desire, we should explore it as well. When asked to create a similar diagram, with the opposing

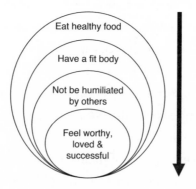

FIGURE 2.6 Kai's Exploration of Core Wants

wants at the top (eating unhealthy food and not exercising), Kai created three sets of circles (Figure 2.7). All three show why he might have been strongly invested in continuing his unhealthy habits.

The first circle tells us what we learned in the section on physiological detours—that food made Kai feel comforted and loved. So, the first step Kai had to take was to find other ways of feeling comforted and loved (playing with his dog, practicing guitar, calling a friend). The other two circles showed additional reasons why he was invested in eating unhealthy food and not exercising. The middle set of circles showed that eating less would diminish the connection to his mother, given she liked to cook for him. Until he found another way to be connected to her (other than going over to her place to eat the very rich meals she prepared), he would not be able to tackle the issue of the body. Finally, his outer-layer want of not exercising appeared to be linked to his early experience of his father forcing him to go running with him. He felt pressured to do it and felt judged throughout their time together. (For Kai's full Wheel of Self, please see the Appendix.)

The combination of the two factors—an outer desire unrelated to multiple core wants and strongly active opposing wants—are

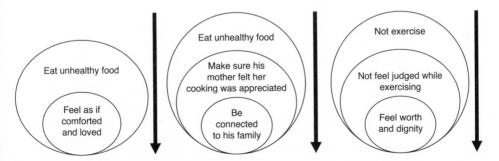

FIGURE 2.7 Kai's Exploration of Opposing Wants

powerful motivational barriers to change. Remember Abhinav, the physiotherapist who struggled in his attempts to work less? His first try at making a diagram (Figure 2.8) looked very logical—he wanted to work less to spend more time with his family. It was a one-layer, thematically related diagram. But when asked to do the "opposing want" exercise, something interesting emerged (see the right set of circles of Figure 2.8).

Abhinav had grown up in a family that struggled financially. He had often witnessed both his father and mother making extreme sacrifices to make sure Abhinav and his brother were not hungry or in need of school supplies. Working less felt like a betrayal of all the sacrifices they have made. Abhinav felt that overworking and sacrificing in his own profession showed his parents that he appreciated all they had done for him over the years. Without having learned how to express gratitude and love toward his parents in a different way, Abhinav would have continued to struggle with overworking for years. (For Abhinav's full Wheel of Self, see the Appendix.)

The work before us, then, is to learn to cut through the associative fog to find core wants that may have been invisible to us for years and discover direct and healthy ways to act on them. As we do that, we need to remind ourselves of two things: to remain grateful for

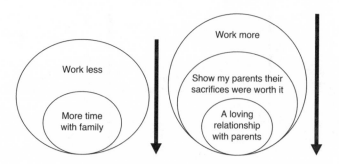

FIGURE 2.8 Abhinav's Exploration of Core Wants

wants that we have already fulfilled in our lives, and to remember that exploring our individual potential is not an exercise in selfishness but a way to bring our very best to our communities.

Why Be Grateful?

We want the most in the domains of our life where we are least satisfied, and these wants can often dominate our attention. So, if we suffer from professional stagnation while at the same time having supportive relationships, it's the wants related to our work that would occupy our minds. This is reasonable given that the mind has evolved to dwell on complex problems until they are resolved, which is a useful spur to development.

On the other hand, our fulfilled wants may become invisible to us. Often, the part of our life that works well can fade into the mental background. This is what is usually meant by the expression "taking things for granted." In the example from earlier in the chapter, our preoccupation with work could make us neglect our family or friends. The danger of taking things for granted is that, in our eagerness to satisfy our unfulfilled wants, we may start to withdraw time or energy from the parts of our lives that are going well and so complicate and slow the developmental process. As our fulfilled wants become invisible, we start taking them for granted (Figure 2.9).

The practice of gratitude, making our fulfilled wants more visible to us, is a powerful means of preserving and protecting things that are already going well in our lives and cultivating both the inner strength and insights necessary for continued development. It is no wonder that studies show the skill of gratitude as a quintessential human strength[9] and a predictor of hope and happiness.[10] Gratitude allows us to systematically remind ourselves to continue giving energy to parts of our lives that are working well.

Wants	UNFULFILLED	FULFILLED
Visible	DEVELOPMENT	GRATITUDE
Invisible	LOST POTENTIAL	TAKING FOR GRANTED

FIGURE 2.9 Invisible and Visible Wants

One more state in Figure 2.9 needs exploring—lost potential. Perhaps a better name for it would be "tragedy." We have associated (all the way since the ancient Greeks) tragedy with death. Yet tragedy is perhaps better linked not to a loss of life but a loss of potential. Losing one's grandmother, who had lived a full life and died at 98, need not be tragic. It may be sad, tender, or poignant. Losing a child in an accident is tragic, for it's a loss of life that could have been, a potential that is lost. Not only a loss of life but a loss of potential in all various forms (relational, intellectual, creative) will strike us as tragic. Our exploration of core wants is meant to make our potential visible. Once visible, it can be a spur to our development.

Despite the modern preoccupation with potential, we often remain unconscious of the core wants that will lead to its fulfillment. The accompanying anxiety and psychological pain make us easy prey to fads, addictions, and advertisers. It is this feeling, in fact, that could be feeding the vast economic empires that lock onto our fears of aging and death. Without fulfillment, and feeling uncertain about how to pursue it, we may be tempted to "buy" ourselves more time. Having more time, unfortunately, will not help us if we don't learn how to read the complex web of our unfulfilled desires. We would just have more years of remaining unfulfilled.

Is It Selfish to Focus On Our Wants?

One final question we may have before exploring our unfulfilled core wants is whether focusing on them is inherently selfish. We don't need to worry. The striking thing about human core wants is just how many of them are relational and communal in nature. We want to build relationships with friends, lovers, and colleagues. We want to build communities not just around our families of origin but around interests, intellectual pursuits, and grand human endeavors possible only with the help of many other humans—both living and dead. We thrive through the community transfer of knowledge and wisdom that allows us the benefit of not having to reinvent the wheel every single generation.

So, when we see others who compulsively accumulate resources (like money or power) we are not witnessing people who are moved from their core wants but, instead, we are witnessing those laboring on the outer edges of their desires. The obsessive effort invested into distorted constructs (such as that power will bring us safety, or that money will give us worth) is likely to produce destructiveness of self, others, and community resources. Exploring our core wants, therefore, can provide protection against the egoism of unconscious pursuits we fall into at the outer layers of our desires. *Our individual potential is communal at its very core.*

TECHNIQUE 1: REDISCOVERING DESIRES

For those of you who would like to use this book as a guide to development, now is the time to apply some of the concepts we talked about in this chapter. Here, and at the end of each following chapter, you will find techniques: these will include step-by-step instructions, complete with illustrative examples.

STEP 1 (Identify the want/s): *Reflect on what it is that you want the most. Write it down on the outermost circle of Figure 2.10.*

It should be something you have wanted for a while, without which you feel your life would not be fulfilled. You can be unabashed and write without placing constraints on your desires (such as what from our current perspective would be "realistic" to want, or wording it in a way that would be acceptable to others).

Example: Let's say that we want to live until we are 100 years of age. We may think of it as impossible, absurd, or embarrassing to want, but since it's our burning desire to live to 100, that's what we will put down in our outermost circle (Figure 2.10).

STEP 2 (Explore the want/s): *Work your way downward, toward the center of the circle, by asking yourself:* **What do you think you'll have or feel once you satisfy your want?**

What you are looking for is another want, rather than an explanation or rationalization. As we descend layers, we are not asking the

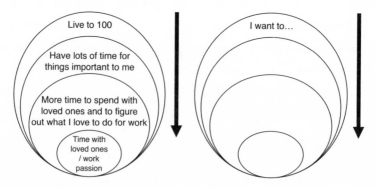

FIGURE 2.10   Technique 1a: Exploring Core Wants

question "Why do you want?" but "What do you want even more intensely?" You can have more than one core want at the center.

Example: Once we know we want to live until 100 (the outer edge of Figure 2.10), we may ask ourselves, "What do I think I'll have or feel if I get to 100?" and respond, "I'll have lots of time to do all the things I don't have time for right now." Then we'd put "Lots of time for things important to me" in the middle circle. Once again, we would ask ourselves, "If I have lots of time for everything, what will I have or feel?" The answer may be something like "I'll have time to connect better with my family and more time to find out what work I'm passionate about." We then place "Connect with family" and "Find work passion" in the center circle. Notice that if you had asked yourself the question why, you may have ended up with an explanation—for example, "I want to live to 100 because it's normal for humans to want to live longer." Instead, by asking what we hope to have or feel if we satisfy our want, we end up with a deeper, more central want.

How will you know that you have arrived at the core want(s)? Chances are you won't exactly know, but here are some things that can guide us. Outer layers frequently include things that are only partially in our control (for example: (a) have others respect our work, (b) find a partner, (c) have children, (d) live to 100). The core wants, on the other hand, are a *desired state of self*, and are therefore much more under our control (for example: (a) be creative in our workplace, (b) be loving to self and others, (c) nurture children in our lives, (d) do our best to age in a healthy manner). If you have arrived at a layer you suspect is a core want but the fulfillment of it depends mostly on others or circumstances in the world, try exploring a bit more.

STEP 3 (Explore opposing/destructive wants): *Ask yourself "What is it that I want or do that has prevented me from fulfilling my core want(s) in the past?" Place it on the outer layer of Figure 2.11 and*

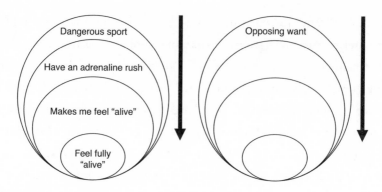

FIGURE 2.11   Technique 1b: Exploring Opposing Wants

repeat steps 1 and 2 to reach core wants. Remember that no matter how destructive the wants on the outer layer may be (for example, Kai eating junk food or Abhinav working more and more), at their center they have core developmental wants, meant to grow you and your relationship with others and the world.

Example: Despite wanting to live to 100, we may want to engage in sports that are dangerous, such as snorkeling in shark-infested waters or skiing in regions where avalanches are frequent. Rationally, we know our actions oppose our desire for long life, but we have a very strong want to do it nonetheless. We would put "Engage in dangerous or life-threatening sport" at the outermost layer and then work our way down as before. What do we want to get or feel when we engage in dangerous sports? We want an adrenaline rush. What do we want from the adrenaline? To feel more alive, which we don't feel when doing our daily routines. The core desire then is "to feel fully alive," and it is indeed something that is a state of self, which we can work on.

STEP 4 (**Choose what to focus on**): *Pick one core want you would want to see fulfilled by the time you are done reading the book.*

You can practice techniques in this book on any of the core wants you discovered. However, it may be best if you pick one as you work through the rest of the techniques in the book. Once you know how to apply techniques with one want, you can go back and repeat the process with the rest.

Example: We now choose a core want that feels most urgent— let's say "discovering work passion." Although other wants (such as improving relationships with family and feeling fully alive) are as important, we feel most urgent about our desire to find work we are passionate about and, therefore, choose to tackle this first.

Exploring wants is a complex, difficult, and highly individual process. Unlike a mathematical or scientific equation, this kind of exploration doesn't have one "right" answer. Whatever wants you find at the center of your circles is the place to start your development. And no matter what you decide you want to change in yourself, simply discovering and acknowledging it is an essential first step to change.

CHAPTER THREE

BEHAVIOR

Now that we have done the difficult work of finding the core wants, what are we to do next? Why not simply find healthy one-layer constructs that will lead us to their fulfillment and just "do it"? Why should we hesitate to directly satisfy our core wants by changing behavior? Because *when we are stuck in some part of our life, the blocks to change extend not just to wants but to emotions, mind, and body too, which makes behavioral change difficult to sustain.*

Kai knew that a one-layer path to a healthy body was eating well and exercising, but forcing himself to do it didn't work for long. Emily knew that picking up art supplies and drawing was always available to her, but she couldn't get herself to do it. Even after the exploration of his wants, Abhinav knew he could simply stop taking on new clients but ended up always taking on more. The mental, emotional, and old neural blocks were pushing against behaviors that would fulfill them.

Rather than launch us into action, the purpose of our work in this chapter is to *restore enough willpower to move the rest of the Wheel of Self* (Figure 3.1). What that means is that, paradoxically, our task will be to *do less* and sometimes even *do nothing*. Doing less of what hasn't worked in the past will help us restore willpower, to give us enough energy to continue our inner work. But to understand how

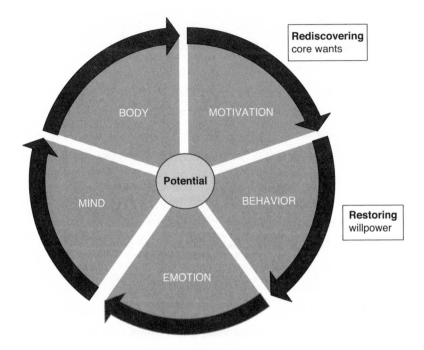

FIGURE 3.1   The Wheel of Self Techniques

behavior works in relation to willpower and how to restore ourselves, we must step back and look at the whole Wheel of Self again.

Any behavior—let's say, getting up from the chair to go to the fridge and make a sandwich—is caused by other parts of the self: motivations, emotions, thoughts, and the old patterns carried in the body. We could be motivated by hunger (motivation), feel anxious and want to be comforted by food (emotions), or think about the pickles we bought yesterday (mind). It could also be that time of the day when we usually get ourselves a sandwich, and our body is following an old routine. Notice how behavior is activated by all other parts of the self.

It is no surprise, then, that when we attempt to change something about ourselves—such as trying to eat better, exercise more, become more assertive, or build better relationships—focusing on changing only the behavior without moving other parts of the self frequently results in self-defeat. We will have employed our willpower to push one spoke of the wheel in one direction, while the rest of the wheel's momentum is going in the opposite direction. It is no surprise that after a while we feel drained and broken. Using willpower on any (or all) *other parts of the self* is likely to be more effective. So why is it that we don't do that? Because behavior is the most visible part of the self, and using our willpower on behavior is not complicated. We just force ourselves to do something. To use willpower to change emotions, mind, and old neural pathways is more complicated and requires more knowledge, and we usually run out of energy before we even begin to explore it.

It makes sense that behavior dominates our field of attention. The social world is built on interacting with others through behaviors (which include both their physical actions and words), and those have direct and immediate effects on us. No matter what people want, think, or feel, we have to deal with the consequences of their actions. Only in close relationships, and perhaps through the arts, do we gain access to others' inner lives, and even that is through a foggy lens, which leads us to believe they are more like us than they really are.[1]

We often interpret our observations of others' behavior in a way that suits us. For example, when people say something that we find offensive, we rarely consider their inner life—all their wants, thoughts, emotions, and past experiences—that may have caused them to act that way. Instead, we reason backward from behavior to trait; if they hurt us, they must be bad people.[2] It's the kind of reasoning we rarely apply to our own behavior. After all, we are vividly aware of contradictions and misalignments within ourselves.

Given that behavior is the most socially visible and understood part of the self, it is natural that when we want to change, it is the behaviors we target. When we fail, behaviors make it obvious that we failed. Most of us use willpower indiscriminately on behaviors we want to control and only pay attention to the process when things don't go well; for example, when we relapse into old behaviors or approach burnout. Using willpower on behaviors is energetically the most expensive option since it doesn't yield changes to the whole self-system. Instead, it keeps us stuck in a state of fragmentation, our different parts pulling in different directions.

A central goal of this chapter will be to help us understand the economy of willpower so that *we can restore it sufficiently to move emotions, mind, and old neural pathways in a new direction.* To do so, we must challenge some basic assumptions about the best path to fulfill our desires and resist the urge to force our behaviors to change. What we want is to make sustained movement in the whole Wheel of Self so that our new way of being will continue naturally and not require either habit or willpower to maintain over time. It will be simply our natural, new way of being.

To restore ourselves, we will have to understand how we earn, spend, and save precious energy for change—our willpower.

THE ECONOMY OF WILLPOWER

Willpower is what psychologists call **self-regulation**—an ability to force ourselves to do what we don't want to do (like go for a run at 6:00 a.m. on a cold winter morning) or restrain ourselves from doing what we do want to do (have a doughnut to get us through a late-night meeting).[3] On the contrary, doing what we want (watching a movie) and not doing what we don't want (not cleaning the bathroom) doesn't require any self-regulation. Willpower becomes active when we try to do something different than what our Wheel of Self would *naturally* do. It is an agent of self-change.

While we will now discuss the economy (earning, spending, saving) of willpower, the broader question we may want to answer first is how it is best used. As already mentioned, when we need to activate our stalled Wheels of Self, the most efficient use of willpower is to move emotions, mind, and old neural pathways rather than act directly on behaviors. Once all our Wheels of Self are moving well, we will notice that willpower will no longer be dominating our everyday activities but will retreat into the background, to be used as needed. Natural development doesn't require much willpower to keep us growing.

So how does willpower work? Psychologist Roy Baumeister and his colleagues researched how self-regulation impacts behavior. The results showed that if people are asked to do a task they don't want to do and then, right after, another task they also don't want to do, they fail faster at the second task. For example, if we force ourselves to do boring paperwork at our job, we'd have less willpower to force ourselves to skip an unhealthy treat immediately after the task.

Baumeister's research shows this effect across different behaviors. One of his studies showed that individuals instructed not to eat chocolate cookies in front of them (which requires willpower for most of us) were then less able to persist in solving unsolvable puzzles.[4] In another study, those instructed to control their emotional expression (not smile) while watching a funny movie (which also needs willpower) showed less mental stamina in subsequent tasks.[5] Not just mental but also physical stamina (our handgrip strength) is affected when we are trying to exercise willpower. The more willpower we use, the less of it we have for other things.[6]

The conclusion of Baumeister and his colleagues was that self-regulation works like a muscle—there is only so much strength we have at any particular time, and the more demands we have on it, the less well it will work. The metaphor of the muscle works the other way around too. The more we exercise our willpower, the more the muscle is strengthened and the more self-regulation we'll have over time.

Another metaphor that works well is that of a cup. Let's say we wake up in the morning with a cup full of willpower and pour out a little bit every time we do something we don't want to do. Remember Kai from the last chapter? He had frequently tried to use his will-power to maintain healthy eating and exercise behaviors. At 6:00 a.m., when his alarm would wake him, he would get out of bed even if he was very tired. Then he would make a green smoothie (at the recommendation of his nutritionist), which he strongly disliked but drank anyway. Kai would then go to the gym and spend an hour doing exercises prescribed by his personal trainer. Although he didn't mind going to the gym (he liked to walk there) and liked stretching, he found strength training unpleasant and painful. Once he was back home, Kai would shower, change, pack his healthy lunch, and go to work. By the time he arrived at work at 8:30 a.m., he would have already poured a lot of willpower out of his cup. Now he had to navigate colleagues, bosses, and projects. If the day went well, he was likely to stick to his healthy lunch and may even have gotten home with some willpower left to complete the day healthfully.

But if the day hadn't gone well—if he had quarreled with one of his friends, had a difficult work interaction, or one of his parents had a health emergency—his cup of willpower would have emptied rapidly. This is when he would forget about the healthy lunch he left in the office fridge and find his way to the burger place a block away. Once there, with no willpower left in the cup, he'd indulge in his favorite burger, fries, and soda, while feeling guilty and defeated. He'd then promise himself to get back to his healthy routine as soon as the disturbance or crisis he encountered had passed.

Notice that Kai was doing what is energetically the most expensive thing to do—using willpower to try to control and change his behaviors rather than working on other parts of the self. Yet even after he learned that using willpower on emotions, mind, or old patterns was more effective, he still didn't have sufficient self-regulation to do it. Without sufficient willpower, we can't change our natural or spontaneous way of being (whether just our behaviors or the whole Wheel of Self). Therefore, we need to understand how we spend, earn, and save (economize) willpower and learn to restore ourselves enough to effectively restart the Wheel of Self by working on emotions, mind, and old neural pathways.

The first, counterintuitive, thing for Kai to do was to *stop most of the things he was forcing himself to do* to save his willpower (Figure 3.2). (The complete Technique 2 for restoring willpower is described at the end of this chapter.) The second step he had to take was to keep parts of his healthy routine that didn't require willpower—that he enjoyed naturally. This meant he started getting up an hour later (around 7:00 a.m.) and walked to the gym (which he enjoyed). Once there, he would do stretches (which he also liked) and then walk back.

---

1. Please list "overdoing" and forced behaviors that you think will rapidly bring you to your desired outcome.

- Waking up at 6:00 a.m.
- Exercising
- Green smoothies for breakfast
- Healthy lunch

STOP

---

2. Pick a few behaviors in the domain of your desire that you enjoy doing (that don't require any willpower).

- Walking to the gym and back
- Stretching at the gym
- Including fruit with my breakfast

CONTINUE

FIGURE 3.2   Kai's Analysis of Overdoing and Developmental Behaviors

For breakfast, he would skip the green smoothie but added fruits, which he enjoyed eating.

This stopping of forced behavior is often the most challenging part of moving the Wheel of Self. Most of us have spent many years forcing ourselves into new or healthy behaviors, and stopping many of them feels like giving up or failing. Also, when we are highly invested in the result, we often **overdo** and try to change many behaviors all at once. For example, if we decide we want to start dating, we may sign up for three different dating apps, join a club, start new hobbies, and go out with friends most evenings of the week. The sheer volume of what we are trying to do will deplete us. Without refocusing our willpower, restoring it, and redeploying it away from behavior and toward emotions, mind, and old neural patterns, it will be difficult to move the Wheel of Self.

The time and energy Kai saved by not forcing himself to do things he didn't want to do or overdoing behaviors were reinvested to further restore himself. The last step left for him to do was to figure out what activities pour willpower back into his cup.

Restoring Ourselves

Often, just before we sleep, we feel our cup of willpower has been drained. Yet, in the morning, we wake up with a full cup of energy (if not in burnout) and start pouring it out all over again. What happened is that, overnight, our willpower got restored. Just as a fatigued muscle needs rest to restore strength, sleep restores willpower.[7] Other activities that research has shown to improve self-regulation include exposure to nature (your favorite parks, mountains, lakes, or sea),[8] positive affect (anything that makes you laugh or smile),[9] and meditation. Meditation, in particular, is known to expand the size of the cup of willpower, and it does so over the long term[10]. As little as

11 hours of meditation can increase the network efficiency and neural connectivity in the part of the brain implicated in improved self-regulation.[11]

Even imagining someone else getting restored can increase our willpower (the process known as "vicarious restoration"), but only if we believe the person we are imagining is similar to us.[12] Implicit beliefs about how much willpower we have can also impact how much of it we end up with. Research by psychologist Carol Dweck and her colleagues shows that if we believe we have more willpower, we end up with more; if we believe we have less, we end up with less.[13] We can think of all the things just mentioned as **universal restorers** of willpower—things that are likely to restore everyone.

Finally, all **intrinsically motivated** activities (those engaging core, developmental wants) will also restore our willpower.[14] This gives us a whole host of **unique restorers** of self-regulation—physical (yoga, running, sports, hikes), social (time with friends, family, meeting new people, engaging with social clubs), individual (knitting, reading, watching funny videos, listening to music, taking pets for a walk), creative (playing an instrument, writing, painting, cooking, interesting work projects), or spiritual (praying, reading inspirational books). Any of these, and many more, can pour back into our cup. The key point to remember is that only *we* can know what works best for us because our core wants and potential, our sources of intrinsic motivation, are unique.

An interesting paradox of restoration is that even if the activity takes up physical energy (like playing a sport or going to a yoga class) and makes us tired, it can still refresh and strengthen our willpower. There are also many instances of the same activities being sometimes draining and sometimes restoring, such as taking care of children or working on demanding but interesting projects. What restores us may also change as we age.[15] Whereas reading a novel used to refresh us when we were in our 20s, now it may be a good conversation with a friend or cooking for pleasure. This makes sense given what we know about our motivational system; as we fulfill some aspects of our potential, others open up, requiring a change in developmental direction.

The configuration of states, activities, and interactions that pour back into our cup is truly unique, and it's worthwhile to explore them thoroughly. It would be good for each of you to make a list of at least seven of your **unique restorers** and keep it at hand. Keeping them accessible will help you apply them when you need it the most. Restorers tend to differ in the time it takes to do them—some are as short as a few minutes (listening to a favorite song), others take at least an hour (going to a yoga class, getting together with friends), while still others require extensive planning and time resources (traveling to another country). Having your restorers easily accessible will help you use them to pour back into your cup when you most need it.

Here is Kai's list of his intrinsically motivated restorative activities: playing with his dog, watching 15 minutes of a show by his favorite comedian on his phone, talking to friends, taking a walk, playing video games, chatting with his colleagues about interesting projects, and traveling. Kai pinned the list on the screensaver of his phone so that he could be reminded to continue pouring back into his cup whatever he could, even for just 10-to-15 minutes. The aim was to restore as much as possible so he could continue the inner change work on emotions, mind, and old neural pathways.

Even if you are not working on restoring yourself as a part of trying to move the Wheel of Self (as Kai was doing), having the restorers at hand and engaging in them regularly will keep you energized and prevent a slide into burnout.

Burnout

What happens if we continue to pour out of our willpower cup without pouring in and continue doing it for a long time? We risk

burnout. When in burnout, we are physically exhausted, motivationally disengaged, mentally foggy, and feeling helpless, all of which makes us inefficient at whatever task we choose to do[16] (Figure 3.3).

We may have difficulty getting out of bed, be disinterested not just in our work but in whatever else used to bring us joy, and feel either numb or a flood of negative emotions. At work, our thinking may be foggy, and tasks that used to take us 15 minutes to complete may now take hours. What is happening to us is that our exposure to prolonged stress is affecting our ability to recover from it. Another way to think of it is that burnout is a decrease in the power of restorers to restore us. Let us look at Figure 3.4 to conceptualize this idea.

FIGURE 3.3   Signs of Burnout

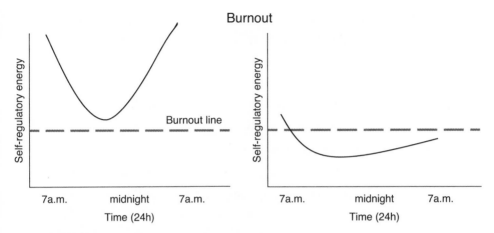

FIGURE 3.4 Conceptualizing Burnout

When not in burnout, our willpower can be represented as a U-shaped curve. We start the day with a cup full of energy, pour out all day by dealing with various stressors and demands of life, and by the time we go to sleep, we are at the bottom of the curve. Sleep (a universal restorer) refills our cup overnight, and in the morning, we start the whole process again. This is a very simplistic version of the complex process of using and restoring willpower during one day-and-night cycle, but it highlights the importance of managing the balance of drainers and restorers in our life.

What happens if we start experiencing significantly more stressors, start forcing ourselves to do more things (as we often do when we try to change), and continue doing so for an extended period? Whereas before burnout, we would wake rested after having a good night's sleep, now we wake up tired. Before the burnout, a week-long vacation would help us deeply restore and prepare for months of intense work. After the burnout, we feel drained two days after returning from vacation. Before the burnout, doing yoga, meeting friends, or reading a novel gave us lots of pleasure. After burnout, everything seems tiring.

Chronic stress impairs the functioning of the hypothalamic-pituitary-adrenal (HPA) axis, which is crucial in helping us recover from stress.[17] This declining ability to be restored is a defining aspect of burnout and has serious implications. It is as if our willpower cup has a crack at the bottom, so no matter how much we pour in, we never seem to refill it. Just pouring in restorers is no longer enough, and we need to fix the cup; that is, to let our body recover its ability to restore us. While in burnout, we require a much more drastic rebalancing of drainers and restorers than what we would need while trying to prevent it.

While we tend to think of drainers as stressful situations and restorers as rejuvenating activities, burnout will force us to a more radical examination of both. Often this means not just reducing stressors and restoring more but transforming how we think and feel about ourselves, others, and the world. Why did we feel we had to ignore a host of burnout symptoms that were slowly becoming visible in our lives? Why did we feel we had to "push through"? Is being burnt out becoming a norm in our society? These are not just individual questions but societal ones as well. It may be time to rethink our collective strategy of living at the edge of our self-regulatory resources and always scraping the bottom of our cup. Not asking these questions is dangerous to individuals and societies alike. A body whose ability to recover is impaired, if placed under further stress, has nowhere to go but to illness, and both individuals and societies suffer the consequences.[18]

Is More Willpower Always Better?

When reflecting on willpower, many of us may believe that all our problems in life could be solved by simply having more. After all, willpower is called a "power" for a reason. It is not lost on us that if we can wake up earlier than everyone else, bear the terrible morning commute with equanimity, smile at the colleagues we dislike, eat our kale salad, exercise on our lunch break, work on projects we may find boring, engage in difficult negotiations with low blood sugar, and then go home and have the patience to help our kids with their homework, we will be almost superhuman. While at it, why not use evenings to work on additional certifications and courses that will help our career along? We may believe that with unlimited willpower, all our human constraints would fade into the background. The muscle metaphor subtly encourages this view: the more, the better.

Yet the fantasy of unlimited willpower has its shadows. It is true that many of us live at the very edge of our self-regulatory capacity, so when something unexpected and troubling happens, it may push us over the edge. Then we may not have enough willpower to go to the gym, not light up a cigarette, or not eat that third slice of pizza. From this perspective, self-regulation is there to prevent self- and other-destructive behaviors. And indeed, in the short term, it can function that way. Like taking a painkiller for a headache, self-regulation can help us get through the moment without causing damage to ourselves and others. Yet believing willpower is an unequivocal force for good in our lives is misleading.

If we believed that most of our core wants and intrinsic impulses are destructive (agreeing with Tennyson that our nature was "red in tooth and claw," or with Freud that sexual and aggressive impulses dominate our unconscious), then it would also make sense to believe that we can achieve our true humanity only through the civilizing force of willpower. The central premise of this book, however, is that while we *can* become destructive at the periphery of our desires, at our very core, we are curious, creative, relational, and intellectual, and we are pulled toward fulfillment by a developmental process that is intrinsically motivated.

When we are at our best and developing the most, willpower will function not at the center of our life activities but at its periphery. It means that most of the things we do in the day will be those we *want* to be doing, and only some of our time will we be forcing ourselves to do things we don't like. For example, even if we love our work, occasionally we'll have to force ourselves to do some boring paperwork. Even the most fulfilling relationship will have occasional troubles. Here fulfillment is at the center and willpower is at the periphery.

What happens if willpower is at the very center of our lives? It points to a bigger problem. When our self-regulatory load is heavier than usual—if we are in a job we hate, in a relationship we have outgrown, or are overly extended in our caregiving duties—all the daily acts of willpower would ensure we are feeling continually drained. This means that the more willpower we have available, the more we are in danger of bearing (and stagnating in) difficult and draining situations. The pain of utter depletion may be the self-system's stern warning that our lives need to change. Of course, the pain of the willpower lapse is only one route to changing our life circumstances, but it's an important one. We must remind ourselves that unlimited willpower would allow us to live and continue living the life we possibly hate.

Willpower is a necessary ingredient to change, but whether it will improve our lives or aid in its stagnation depends on how we use it. If we use it to stay in destructive circumstances, it may destroy us. If we use it to control our behaviors, it will drain us while keeping us at war with ourselves. And if we use it to move the whole Wheel of Self to restart our development, as we hope to do in this book, it may give us a natural developmental momentum to keep moving without requiring willpower at every step. As with all wheels that are stuck or at rest, it takes the most energy to get them going. The techniques described in this book are meant to get the Wheel of Self moving again and let the natural developmental process keep it rolling along. When that happens, we will continue to use willpower, but not at the center of our lives. Rather, we will use it at the periphery—to support our intrinsically motivated development.

THIEVES OF TIME AND ENERGY

The last task we have as we try to fully restore ourselves is to identify whether we engage in activities that we think of as restorers that are really **distractors**. They are activities that distract us from underlying negative states and emotions (restlessness, boredom, anxiety, etc.). For example, scrolling social media feeds throughout our workday may feel good simply because it diverts our attention from a stressful work environment. Notice that it won't give us energy and may do just the opposite. It only distracts rather than restores.

How would we be able to tell the difference between a distractor and a restorer? To understand that, we need to monitor our energy as we come out of the activity. Do we feel mentally and emotionally energized or more tired? Did we indulge in it far longer than necessary for the supposed objective (getting informed)? We also need to know what our favorite distractors are. What is the first thing we do when we feel stressed, anxious, or restless? Is it scrolling news, browsing Instagram, hitting the fridge, or opening a bottle of wine? By adulthood, most of us have accumulated a few favorite ways to distract ourselves; upon reflection, we are likely to know what they are.

Notice that the very same activity can act both as a restorer and distractor when engaged for a different reason. When Kai played video games because he was excited about the new game (he liked exploratory, problem-solving ones), he would end up feeling refreshed and restored. But when he was procrastinating or feeling restless, he would play for too long, was distracted even while playing, and would end up feeling drained and tired.

The last step of Kai's restoration technique (Fig 3.5) was to identify his distractors and start engaging his restorers instead. This is what his full chart of restoration looked like.

Notice that while distractors don't usually require any willpower (since they provide immediate relief from the pain of negative emotion), it is for the same reason they can become addictive and, because they take away time from restorers, an energy drain. Indulging the distractors over a long period of time prevents us from restoring,

1. Please list "overdoing" and forced behaviors that you think will rapidly bring you to your desired outcome.

- Waking up at 6:00 a.m.
- Exercising
- Green smoothies for breakfast
- Healthy lunch

STOP

2. Pick a few behaviors in the domain of your desire that you enjoy doing (that don't require any willpower).

- Walking to the gym and back
- Stretching at the gym
- Including fruit with my breakfast

CONTINUE

3. On the left, please list distractors you engage in when feeling restless, anxious, frustrated, etc. On the right, list your restorers (activities that reenergize you).

DISTRACTORS	RESTORERS
• Comfort eating	• Playing with the dog
• Scrolling social media feeds	• Watching videos of favorite comedian
• Video games (out of restlessness)	• Talking to friends
	• Chatting to colleagues about projects
	• Video games (when fully engaged)

REPLACE

FIGURE 3.5   Kai's Chart of Restoration

which pours back into our cup. This danger plays itself out continually in our lives. For example, we come home from a stressful day at work and know that we need rest. Yet, we keep scrolling through the news or social media late at night. It doesn't energize us, and for a short time, it's energy neutral, but the longer we do it, the more we will feel drained and depleted. The final step of our restoration process is to replace distractors with restorers.

Let's look at another example to see what restoration would look like in action. Aisha was a 32-year-old engineer who wanted to advance to a leadership position in her organization. Although occasionally feeling like an imposter and not deserving of her position, she still felt her skills were superior to those who were promoted above her. After being passed over for promotion twice, she was told by her boss she didn't have leadership "presence," that she appeared timid and unsure in meetings, and that she would need to gain more leadership skills before being given the promotion. Aisha suspected that some of her boss's reluctance to promote her was due to her being one of the few women of color in her company, but she couldn't be sure. She couldn't trust her instincts, so instead she took what he said at face value and tried to work on her "presence."

Aisha thought of the feedback in behavioral terms. She gave herself the task of speaking up at every meeting at least three times, no matter how uncomfortable she felt. She showed up at work earlier than her colleagues and stayed later; kept answering emails on evenings, weekends, and holidays; and volunteered for new projects that came along. She forced herself to do all these things, getting more and more depleted with time. Although Aisha felt drained, she thought she would finally recover once she was promoted. Aisha was **overdoing**—trying desperately to reach her goal of being promoted by applying willpower to her behaviors. Yet all that her activity produced was being drained and overburdened by projects.

Note that when we are in the overdoing mode, our activity will be frenzied, not properly gauged and directed. The renewed commitment to the plan and the confidence that "this time it will work" is likely to be fragile. We may begin to execute our plan with rigid adherence and subjugate all other aspects of our life to it. Still, after an impressive but short burst of activity or a prolonged teeth-clenching effort, we may lose momentum.

When she was not working too hard, Aisha spent the little free time she had scrolling through LinkedIn profiles of people who were in the positions she coveted, trying to understand how they got to their roles. Usually, that would make her feel even more drained, and she would call up her friends or family members, complaining of her situation at work, or order pizza and watch reruns of her favorite TV shows late into the night. Her sleep suffered, and sometimes she would wake up at 4:00 a.m. and, unable to fall back asleep, check her emails and try to do work before starting the day again. These were her **distractors**, and they left her no time to truly restore herself.

Different people have different ways to distract themselves. One person may get on social media and check for likes on his posts, another will reach for a cigarette, eat when not hungry, or watch TV. *Distractions can be anything that comforts us without restoring us.* We can even distract ourselves through activities that, from the outside, seem very productive (such as exercise, travel, work, or reading). The key is to notice whether we are engaging in them to get away from our feelings of restlessness, boredom, or anxiety, or because we intrinsically want to exercise, work, or travel, which can be developmental and restorative.

Aisha started her inner work by completing Technique 1 (Rediscovering Desires) and located her core desires: feeling self-worth and being able to create and contribute to her organization with confidence. Moving on to the "Behavior" part of the Wheel of Self, she had to restore enough willpower to continue the work on emotions, mind, and body. She now needed to do something very difficult: to stop doing. First, she had to identify all behaviors she forced herself to do because she thought they will help her reach her aim and *stop* them. She also had to *continue* a few behaviors in the direction of her core wants she found intrinsically rewarding (and therefore required no willpower to maintain). Finally, she had to identify her distractors and *replace them with restorers*. We can see her full chart on restoring willpower in Figure 3.6.

1. Please list "overdoing" and forced behaviors that you think will rapidly bring you to your desired outcome.

- Speaking at least three times every meeting
- Arriving to work early, the last to leave work
- Answering emails in the evenings, on the weekends, and on holidays
- Volunteering for extra projects suggested by her bosses

STOP

2. Pick a few behaviors in the domain of your desire that you enjoy doing (that don't require any willpower).

- Arriving to work early
- Trying to empty the email inbox by 6:00 p.m. and then leaving it until the next morning
- Volunteering for projects that are of special interest to me

CONTINUE

3. On the left, please list distractors you engage in when feeling restless, anxious, frustrated, etc. On the right, list your restorers (activities that reenergize you).

DISTRACTORS	RESTORERS
• Scrolling through LinkedIn profiles of colleagues	• Researching new technologies in the field
• Watching TV reruns	• Watching interesting films
• Comfort eating	• Exploring new restaurants with friends
• Complaining to friends and family members	• Learning new languages

REPLACE

FIGURE 3.6 Aisha's Chart of Restoration

Notice that Aisha kept some of her old behaviors, such as going to work early, trying to get her inbox cleared by 6:00 p.m., and volunteering for projects that were of particular interest to her. They didn't require any willpower since she enjoyed doing them. What she stopped doing was all the extra behaviors she had forced herself into just to impress her bosses. That saved her a lot of willpower and set her on the path of restoration. Finally, once she identified her distractors (scrolling LinkedIn, comfort eating, TV reruns, etc.) and started replacing them with her restorers (researching new technology in her field, watching interesting films, exploring new restaurants with friends, etc.), she started to feel less drained and depleted.

Stopping her old ways of trying to fulfill her desire allowed Aisha to stop overdrawing from her willpower balance sheet. With every overdoing behavior she stopped and every distractor she replaced with a restorer, her cup of willpower became increasingly full. Soon she was ready to work on other parts of the self that had prevented her from continuing development. Paradoxically, to move the Wheel of Self sustainably, we have to stop behaviors we think will get us directly to our desire. We also need to find and replace distractors that are stealing both our time and ability to restore. It's only when we can restore enough willpower and feel our cup start to refill that we are ready for the next stage of our inner work.

BEYOND HABITS

Before we describe step-by-step how to do Technique 2, we will examine one more question. What does it mean that when we are functioning optimally (when the Wheels of Self are moving well), we use willpower at the periphery of our development but not at its center? The concept of willpower is frequently conflated with that of

self-motivation. *Self-motivation is a state in which we use willpower to support (at the periphery) intrinsically motivated activities.*

Any profession, activity, or relationship, no matter how appealing to us, will have components we don't like. Let's say a basketball player needs to do a hundred push-ups a day as a part of her training. She may love basketball but not the push-ups. With self-motivation, willpower is directed only at some components of the activity. The player doesn't force herself to play basketball but only forces herself to do push-ups, which will support her playing. For every intrinsically motivated activity, at the center there is pouring in (the activity itself) and pouring out (support actions which may be forced). This dynamic restoration and depletion of willpower can happen almost simultaneously. This is why, no matter how demanding, truly loved activities can be pursued vigorously despite the often enormous self-regulatory toll.

Understanding our core wants (see Chapter Two) is crucial to this process because they are the source of intrinsically motivated or developmental activities that restore willpower. Dancers who love their art (and who find that dancing pours into their cup) don't necessarily love getting up at 6:00 a.m. for rehearsals or managing injuries they are likely to suffer during their career. These are issues that surround what is an intrinsically motivated activity. If we work at something we love that develops us, the activity itself will give us more willpower, even if we spend some of it peripherally to support the central activity by doing things we don't necessarily like.

If we find an activity not intrinsically motivating, *all* aspects of it pour *out* of our cup. This, perhaps, is one of the reasons why it's so difficult to excel at activities or professions that we dislike. All the while we are pouring willpower out of our cup, our colleagues, who like the work, are pouring willpower into their cups (even if they dislike some peripheral aspects of the work). This is also why it's so difficult for those who don't like their work to outperform those who do.

What makes motivations "intrinsic" is that they lie at the center of the motivational circles we discussed in Chapter Two. Given the boundlessness of human capacity for development, we can often detect subtle changes in how intrinsically motivating something is by watching how much willpower we have to pour into it. In that way, the cup doesn't lie. If your favorite activity years ago was meeting new and interesting people in large gatherings and now you find these very same gatherings more and more draining, it's worthwhile observing this shift. It means your motivational system is no longer developmentally engaged by socializing in large events. Watching changes in our willpower "consumption" can alert you to meaningful changes in your motivational system and, accordingly, in your development.

What about habits? Aren't they meant to keep our cup full by not engaging our willpower? It turns out that while habits don't consume our willpower, they also don't restore us, and they remain static while our development demands change.

Habits are what we do when we are not thinking about what we should do. Studies show that when under stress or on mindless "autopilot," we are more likely to do whatever we are used to when prompted by our past experiences and situational cues.[19] If we are in the habit of eating no breakfast, we'll eat no breakfast. If we are in the habit of eating a healthy breakfast, that's what we'll do. In a sense, habit is a behavioral sequence we perform without having to be present. It happens by itself. One way to think of it as "encrusted" choices that we made so many times in the past, they happen when we don't have enough energy to attend to the choice.

Given how drained we are most of the time, it makes sense that we have glamorized good habits. We want to know that when we are on autopilot, we are doing the right and healthy thing. The same holds for exercise routines and diets. Most of the self-development advice offered is usually wrapped in sets of prescriptions and schedules that take a lot of willpower because they require changes in behavior. Proponents of habits point out that if these behaviors can be automatized and become energy neutral, it would seem like a big win for not draining the cup of willpower and still doing all the prescribed behaviors that are supposed to be good for us.

The problem is that, while habits (even good habits) remain the same, we are in a continual state of flux. Our body may need more protein one morning and more fiber another. If we are always eating the same breakfast on autopilot, we are not likely to notice or respond to it.

Psychologist Ellen Langer's seminal research on mindfulness shows that it is not the rigid application to schedules but the mindfulness to variability in the self that causes real improvements in human functioning.[20] An asthma patient told to take two doses of an inhaler, one in the morning and one in the evening, is advised that this prescription works well (on average) for thousands of others with similar symptoms. Yet, none of us is actually "average." On the contrary—when patients are encouraged to monitor the variability of their symptoms and use the inhalers when necessary, they are more likely to reduce their own asthma symptoms.[21] Improving mindfulness also improves learning,[22] reduces stress,[23] reduces alcoholism,[24] improves life expectancy among the elderly,[25] and reduces physical symptoms and improves well-being in patients suffering from terminal neurodegenerative disease.[26] Why is that?

While a good habit is better than a bad habit, mindfulness and responsiveness to the self are even better than a good habit. Of course, those of us who feel drained by our daily demands may find the prospect of sensitivity and mindfulness to the self another effort we'd rather not engage in. On the other hand, building and sticking to habits not responsive to our constantly changing wants could be an even greater loss. We keep some energy but lose our development.

Now that we understand the economy of willpower better, we can think of how to maintain it at healthy levels. What would happen if we reorganized our lives to try to turn, as far as possible, self-regulatory tasks into self-motivated tasks? Let's think of exercise, something many of us don't get enough of. Getting up at 6:00 a.m. to go to the health club to swim laps in the pool may sound like an excellent plan to improve health—except that we may not be morning people, we may hate changing into our swimming gear, or may not even like swimming itself. We know it's great for us, but that doesn't make the activity intrinsic, nor does it pour willpower into our cup. The question we should ask ourselves is why? Why swimming or running; why at 6:00 a.m. or every night? What would happen if we embedded something we love in something we think we should do?

The assignment (for all of us) could be to design a set of activities that would help us reach our health goals by doing intrinsically enjoyable things. It's eating strawberries instead of forcing ourselves to eat kale. It's going for a pickup soccer game in the evening instead of swimming laps in the morning. It does require a bit of creativity and effort to design our life this way and turn self-regulation into self-motivation, but it can be done. By turning forced activities into events that are intrinsically motivated, we can keep pouring back into our cup.

TECHNIQUE 2: RESTORING WILLPOWER

Once you have identified what core want you want to pursue with Technique 1, it's time to recoup the willpower to be able to continue your inner work. Figure 3.7 is the chart that will help you restore it and pour more self-regulatory capacity back into your cup.

1. Please list "overdoing" and forced behaviors that you think will rapidly bring you to your desired outcome.

STOP

2. Pick a few behaviors in the domain of your desire that you enjoy doing (that don't require any willpower).

CONTINUE

3. On the left, please list distractors you engage in when feeling restless, anxious, frustrated, etc. On the right, list your restorers (activities that reenergize you).

DISTRACTORS RESTORERS

REPLACE

FIGURE 3.7   Technique 2: Restoring Willpower

STEP 1: *List "overdoing" behaviors that you force yourself to do in the hope that they will rapidly bring you to your desired outcome. Try to stop overdoing activities.*

This is perhaps the most counterintuitive part of the technique, and the behaviors we outline here are sometimes the most difficult to stop. After all, why not throw ourselves after what we want? Perhaps remembering that we have tried the same approach of directing our willpower directly to behaviors in the past and that it hadn't worked before may encourage us to pause our efforts for a moment and refocus on restoring our willpower.

Example: This includes overexercising, over-dieting, overworking, and any other activity that we are forcing ourselves to do to get to our outcome. For Kai this was early morning strength training and a green smoothie for breakfast, while for Aisha it was forcing herself to speak three times each meeting and being overly available. A good candidate for overdoing activities is anything you've done repeatedly in the past and that has repeatedly not yielded what you wanted.

STEP 2: *Pick (or find) a few behaviors in the domain of your desire that you enjoy doing (which don't require any willpower). Continue doing them.*

Here, you try to keep yourself in the domain of your desire but without effort. No matter how small, one or two behaviors you enjoy and therefore don't feel drained by are best. We should remember that it's something you can do without trying hard; something you find intrinsically pleasurable.

Example: No matter what domain of your life you are trying to change, there is something in it that you likely enjoy, no matter how small. If your core desire has to do with creativity, keep or find a small project that doesn't require effort; if your core want has to do with being healthier, try to find one healthy food or type of movement you enjoy; if you are trying to improve your relationships, pick one thing you enjoy doing with your loved ones. No matter what core want you are working with, some creative reflection will yield an activity that you don't feel you have to force yourself to do. No matter how little, try to find and continue with it.

STEP 3: *Reflect on your distractors—what you do to escape restlessness, anxiety, boredom, stress, or other negative states—and list them on the left. On the right, list activities that restore you. Try to include at least a few activities that don't take more than 10-to-15 minutes. When you notice yourself engaging in distractors, try to replace them with restorers.*

Try not to judge yourself if you find that, despite your intent to replace distractors with restorers, you automatically continue a distracting activity. It will take a bit of time to come up with a "self-alert" system that will help you make a switch.

Example: Distractors are easy to notice, simply because they are so repetitive. You may be checking your social media feed, reading news, or binging on TV shows whenever you feel restless or stressed. While easy to notice, it may be tricky to switch them over to restorers. This is why having a list of your unique restorers handy is so useful. Put the list somewhere visible (on your phone or desktop home screen or pinned to the fridge). Make sure to add to your list both activities that take very little time (like listening to a song, stretching, watching a clip of a funny video, etc.), and activities that take a longer time (going to movies with friends, taking a yoga class, having a long bath, etc.).

While replacing distractors with restorers may be tricky at first, it can be done. When you reach for your phone to check your social media feed, it's a great time to view a clip of your favorite comedian or read a short article about a topic that intrigues you. When you are restless but can't sleep, you may get up and do some stretching. Knowing what distracts and what restores you, you are better able to pour back into your cup of willpower.

If things that drain you during the week are predictable (projects, people, or situations), you can plan for inserting restorative activities just before or after (or both) the draining activity or interaction. It may mean taking a short walk before a difficult meeting, listening to a song we love after (or during) boring paperwork, and so forth. The idea is to keep pouring back into our cup.

Now that you understand restoration principles, you can work on recouping your willpower. As you start restoring and feeling more energized, you may be tempted to go back to the overdoing behaviors. But try not to let the pendulum swing back to where it has been many times before. Instead, use the energy to continue to the next stage of your inner work: reprocessing emotion.

Emotions are signals that tell us where our obstacles, threats, and losses are, and they have evolved to help us navigate the world to better reach our wants. When stuck, however, emotions start signaling to us not about what is before us but about events in our past. In Chapter Four, we explore how to understand emotions, what healthy processing of emotions looks like, and how to reprocess "sticky" emotions to move the Wheel of Self along.

CHAPTER FOUR

EMOTION

It is time to turn our attention to the next section of the Wheel—emotions. **Emotions** are a signaling system that tells us where we stand in relation to our wants. Are we coming closer (positive emotions), or are we running into trouble (negative emotions)? Not only do they signal to us but they also give us energy and prompt us toward what we have to *do* to get closer to what we want.[1] For example, if we are in a dangerous situation (let's say we encounter a wild animal on our camping trip), fear helps alert us to protect ourselves and energizes us to run away, fight, or freeze, depending on the size and speed of the animal. When emotions work well and we interpret their signals correctly, they become our guides in effectively protecting ourselves, overcoming obstacles, grieving our losses, and feeling happiness as we get closer to our wants. However, being stuck in some domain of our life distorts our emotional signals so they become difficult to interpret.

Despite Emily's seemingly perfect life, she kept feeling negative emotions—she was dissatisfied, anxious, and restless. To Emily, her emotions were the problem, not her life. Blaming the signal for telling us something we don't want to hear is a bit like blaming pain for signaling that we have been injured. Though negative emotions have evolved to protect us and get us closer to our wants, we often treat them as the enemy, trying to avoid, suppress, or distract ourselves from feeling them. Emily tried ignoring her emotions and continuing with her life as it was, successful but bare of creative action. Her emotions, however, kept signaling for change.

The very thing we don't want to experience holds the key to achieving our wants. Aisha felt resentment while waiting for her desired promotion and had bouts of debilitating self-doubt. Kai felt persistent shame about his body and was haunted by hopelessness. Abhinav felt guilty if he wasn't overworking and accommodating patients in his always-expanding physiotherapy practice.

Negative emotions were trying to send Emily, Aisha, Kai, and Abhinav signals, yet these were not interpreted accurately. They tried to work on the outside world to make their emotions change, which when we are stuck, does not work. When stalled in some domain of our life, we need to do *the inner work* to course-correct messages coming from emotions so that we can interpret them accurately and have them act as guides to our growth.

When we are stuck in our development, emotions in the domain of chronically unfulfilled wants are likely to be negative, prolonged, intrusive, and difficult to interpret. They may dishearten us or make us anxious, frustrated, hopeless, or ashamed for a long time, and make our daily experience something we want to "get through" rather than "live in." If we want to understand how to intervene in stuck emotions, we first need to understand how they work when the Wheel of Self is moving well.

EMOTIONS ARE RATIONAL

Many emotions we experience daily—such as being happy, sad, afraid, or frustrated—are so familiar to us that we rarely stop to wonder what they are *for*. We know they can be positive or negative, strong or weak, familiar or confusing. We know they can get us into trouble if they are not handled appropriately. We know that if they are negative and persistent, they will make us miserable. Yet, emotions are different from other reactions in the body (such as having indigestion), different from thoughts (like "this fruit is tasty"), behaviors (going to the fridge), or motivations (being hungry). Although emotions can be said to include all four (reactions, thoughts, behaviors, and motivations), what differentiates them is their *function—what they do for us.*

Emotions in mammals evolved as ways to allow animals *to learn consistently to approach rewards and avoid dangers in their environments.* To be able to know what to approach and what to avoid, we need to remember what we encountered and how it turned out. So if we get sick from eating a type of berry, we need to remember the berry so we can avoid it next time. We can see the connection between memory and emotion in the brain: the amygdala, the part of the brain central to processing emotions, is most closely connected to the hippocampus, which is involved in memory. Up to this point, we know that emotions have goals (to get us to our wants); they signal (and we remember the signals) and they then energize us to act. You can see the components of emotion of all mammals in Figure 4.1.

Contrary to our everyday use of the word "emotional," emotions are rational at their very core. When emotions don't work well, we become more irrational. Damage to the amygdala in rhesus monkeys makes them less afraid and causes them to irrationally engage in a host of potentially fatal exploratory behaviors.[2] Damage to the amygdala in humans impairs their decision-making (such as reasoning rationally about money), both in the lab and in real life.[3] In short, if we have problems with processing emotions, we will quickly start to behave irrationally and bring ourselves into danger and financial ruin. Despite the popular view that emotions are opposed to rationality, we need our emotions to function well in order to act rationally.

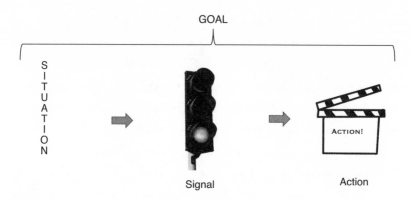

FIGURE 4.1   Components of Emotion in Mammals

In humans, there is an additional component of emotion. Observe Figure 4.2. What you will notice is that between the situation and the signal, there are glasses (lenses) representing our constructs or beliefs (which we talked about in Chapter Two, on motivation). What is this image supposed to represent?

Psychologists Keith Oatley and P. N. Johnson-Laird's influential cognitive theory of emotions placed cognitive appraisals (constructs or beliefs), at the center of our emotional life.[4] That means that when we encounter something in the world, the mind has to interpret it and put it through a "lens" through which we see the situation. The notable exception is a reflexive action in which we first act (jump away from a snake-shaped branch) before the mind catches up and tells us we are not in danger.

For humans, it's the construct or belief that will decide which emotion we'll feel in response to a situation. The very same situation—an environmental disaster, for example—will make some people angry (at climate-change deniers, at politicians), some sad (if they see the situation as bringing about an inevitable loss of life), some fearful (about what will happen to them and their loved ones), and others energized (because they see the situation as an opportunity to reach out helpfully

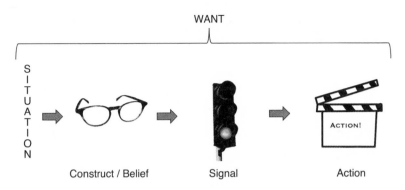

WANT

S
I
T
U
A
T
I
O
N

Construct / Belief   Signal   Action

FIGURE 4.2   All Components of Human Emotion

to the community in trouble). The same situation in different minds will bring about different emotions and, therefore, different actions. In nonhuman mammals, the same situation is likely to always bring about the same emotional response.

An interesting implication of this way of thinking about emotions is that we can't have an emotion without there being a goal or a want. We often believe we simply wake up with emotions, or they come from nowhere, as if they are acquaintances with a key to our house who show up when they want and stay as long as they want. This seeming unpredictability of emotions (particularly negative ones) can make us feel powerless. In reality, *negative emotions come when we veer away from our goals, and they go away as soon as we are back on track to fulfill them.* Emotions are meant to be temporary, as would be logical for a signaling system. A traffic light that is always red or always green would lose its function and purpose.

Uncovering reasons why emotions come when they do, how long they stay, and what they want from us will allow us to let them do the work they were intended for—help us reach our wants. Instead of emotions being acquaintances with a key to our place, unpredictable in their comings and goings, we can treat them as friends who arrive to help us and whose departure we can anticipate after the job gets done.

To be able to show what healthy emotion processing in humans looks like, we first need to address the obvious: If emotions are indeed a rational, learning-based system, how have they acquired such a bad reputation for being irrational? Why do we sometimes make bad decisions when very angry or afraid?

How Did Emotions Get a Bad Reputation?

To help us understand how emotions got a bad reputation, let's look at four basic emotions: anger, fear, sadness, and happiness. Each one is triggered by a different situation (in relation to our goals), and each emotion wants us to do something different that will rationally bring us closer to our goals (Figure 4.3).

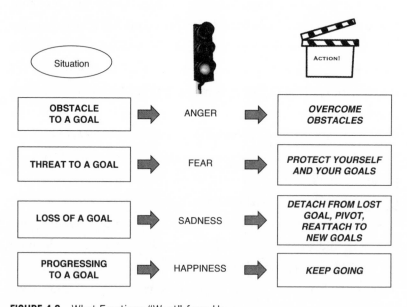

FIGURE 4.3 What Emotions "Want" from Us

So far, this appears rational enough. And it is, for nonhuman mammals, who go from situation to action almost instantaneously. They are helped by the fact that each of the emotions has evolved a corresponding physical "signature" that helps them act. These physical activations are rational for the life of most mammals, who encounter mostly *physical* obstacles, threats, and losses.

Let us look at the physical signatures of fear and anger, where emotions' reputational trouble begins. It is rational that an animal presented with a physical threat or obstacle would recruit all bodily resources for immediate defense, whether for fighting, fleeing, freezing, or trying to commune. This is why we feel an excess of energy when angry or anxious, or even happy (the emotions that require active responses from an evolutionary perspective). While our musculature is fully activated, other less immediately relevant systems, like digestion or cell repair, are deactivated or "put on hold."

In humans, this deactivation of non-urgent bodily systems includes the part of the brain that deals with long-term plans (such as the prefrontal cortex, or PFC).[5] It is entirely rational that, if we are running away from a bear, our long-term plans are irrelevant at that moment. Metaphorically, it's a bit like having a switch at the front of the brain with the tag "PFC," and when we are very angry or afraid, the switch instantaneously goes to an off position so we can deal with what's in front of us. So far, this is a rational response, helping us orchestrate a short-term physical response to a short-term physical problem.

The issue is that, for many of us, our daily threats and obstacles are no longer physical but *psychological*, and many of our goals are *long term*. This means that when we try to tackle a situation with the PFC switch in the off position, terrible things happen. No one would call us irrational for running away from a bear or another physical threat. But if we are sitting at a work meeting and a colleague diminishes us in front of our boss, most people would find that hurling ourselves over the table and tackling him to the ground would be deeply irrational (in addition to getting us arrested). Most of us don't end up in this situation because we use our willpower to turn our PFC switch back on. As we will read later in the chapter, bringing the PFC back online is only the first of multiple steps in effectively processing emotions.

How quickly and thoroughly we turn the switch back on depends on how much we have practiced regulating emotions, the training for which starts in childhood. Notice that even if we don't hurl ourselves physically at the colleague, we may keep the switch in the intermediate position, not committing fully to either on or off. We may give him a nasty look, swear at him in our head, or plan out a terrible email to send him later (and cc the whole company). After some minutes or hours, or perhaps by the next morning, we wake up with the switch back in the on position. Only then, when we fully understand the consequences of our actions on our long-term plans, do we become grateful that the email that would have derailed our entire career remained in the Drafts box. Even in cases in which the threats or obstacles are physical (imagine a police officer during a violent confrontation), the PFC switch needs to be in the on position so that the person can mentally see the long-term consequence of each of their actions.

The reputation of emotions as irrational stems not from the nature of emotions but from changes in the quality of human stressors and the time horizon of our goals. It is exacerbated by observing what happens to us and others in that (hopefully) short period when our PFC switch is still in the off position and we can't bring it back online to orchestrate a rational and long-term response to our obstacles and threats. So next time a driver cuts us off and we are tempted to rear-end them in a flare of road rage, we can't blame emotions for it. Emotions want our PFC to switch back on and our car intact.

Furthermore, when we look at the evolutionary energy "signatures" of sadness and happiness, it's clear they can still assist us with processing our emotions effectively, even with the changes in the nature of our stressors and goals. Low energy associated with sadness is helpful in aiding us to detach from the goal we have lost, whether it's an idea, a job, or a person. The high energy accompanying happiness allows us to progress toward the goal that is getting increasingly closer to fulfillment.

Now that we have understood how emotions ended up suffering undeserved reputational damage, let's talk a bit more about positive emotions. **Happiness**, it turns out, is often mistaken for another positive emotion that is of great significance to our developmental path: **joy**. In the next section, we find what are two different messages that these two different emotions are trying to tell us.

Happiness versus Joy

Let us observe the positive emotion we have discussed up to this point—**happiness**. It is often mistaken for another positive emotion: **joy**. How are happiness and joy different? Happiness signals that we are approaching (or have achieved) a goal, regardless of its kind (if it's core or peripheral; generated internally, by circumstances, or by other people). Joy, on the other hand, is the signal that the *goal we are approaching is a core want that is developing one of our potentials.* Knowing when we feel joy, therefore, can orient us toward development in a way that happiness cannot.

For example, if we are taking a course we don't like, have not prepared for an exam, and cram the night before to get a passing grade, we'll be happy with the outcome (a passing grade) even though there has been zero learning or development. On the other hand, we may feel a continual sense of joy when developing some potential in ourselves, whether it is learning to play guitar, getting to know someone else, or puzzling out a difficult problem, no matter what outcome these activities lead to. Notice that happiness is felt in relation to *outcomes*, comes as a "hit" of positive feelings, and leaves as quickly as it comes. On the other hand, joy is a *continuous signal* that we are in the midst of a *process of development*.

Another difference between joy and happiness is that joy (and development) can coexist with negative states and emotions—such as psychological pain, sadness, or anger. We can approach everything developmentally, including a breakup, the death of a loved one, or the grueling demands of a career we love. Conversely, we can be very happy, fulfilling all the wants on the outside (peripheral) layers of wants, and at the same time feel a profound dissatisfaction and suffering from the lack of development and joy. These seemingly contradictory states tend to be confusing and at the root of the lack of fulfillment that often accompanies worldly successes.

Being process-oriented, joy is one of the rare emotions whose long stay in our psychological "house" doesn't indicate that we are stuck but tells us the opposite: that we are developing.

HOW TO PROCESS NEGATIVE EMOTIONS

Because we are so used to experiencing emotions in the background of our activities, we may get the impression that emotions are there to be "felt." But emotions, if we could give them a voice, would urge us, "Don't just feel me, DO something!" Why? Because most emotions, being energy expensive, have evolved to be temporary and leave as soon as we are on the path to our goal again. So, what are we to do to process emotions in a healthy way?

To answer that question, we need to look at a tool we have at our disposal that our non-human cousins, apes, don't: **choice**. Resilience, the ability to not just cope with troubled circumstances but flourish despite them, can be found in how we leverage this uniquely human tool.

There are two ways you can apply choice: (1) in the moment, when the negative emotion arrives—by learning how to fully **process it** (receive the signal and move to action)—and (2) in the long term, through building **resilience**. We will discuss both in turn.

(Please keep in mind that the following are suggestions on how to process emotions in the domain of our life where our Wheels of Self are moving well. The discussion on how to deal with emotion in the stalled parts of the self is coming up in the sections on sticky emotions and Technique 3.)

In-the-Moment Processing of Negative Emotions

If our Wheel of Self is moving well, how do we process the emotion in the moment—that is, hear its signal and move toward the right action that will lead us to our goal? We could follow these following steps:

1. We approach (NOT suppress/distract/express) and give ourselves space and time to experience it. When a strong negative emotion comes our way, we may not want to deal with it and simply ignore it. If it's particularly strong and impossible to ignore, we may throw ourselves into our favorite distractors (like social media, TV, alcohol, and so on). Another distraction strategy is to immediately enact the primate action tendency (yell or attack when angry, run away from a threat, or withdraw if rejected) and then try to forget about it. None of these options are what is meant by *approach* here. Approaching emotion is giving ourselves space and time to acknowledge what is happening to us and move to the next stage of processing (for example, taking a break during a heated meeting or temporarily leaving a room when we feel too angry during an argument with a spouse).

2. We calm and comfort ourselves (which brings the PFC back online). One metaphor we can use for a strong negative emotion is that it is like a crying baby. It needs to be picked up, calmed down, or comforted before we do anything else. Everyone has a unique way of calming themselves—letting long breaths out, feeling their feet against the floor, or taking a sip of water. If we are at home, we can find additional ways to feel comforted: wrapping ourselves in a blanket, having a hot tea, or journaling—whatever it is that makes us feel grounded, calm, and safe.

How is comforting ourselves different from distracting ourselves (with food, television, etc.)? The difference is that after distraction we will have stopped thinking about our emotions, whereas after comforting ourselves the emotion will still be in our awareness, yet we will feel calm enough to be able to continue processing it. This process of calming and comforting (feeling safe) is what allows our PFC to come back online, which gives us back long-term planning capabilities.

3. We examine what implicit and explicit wants and constructs underlie our emotion(s). It is time to find out which of our goals is being threatened and what exactly triggered the emotion. This ability to calm and orient ourselves in space, time, and situation allows us to start doing what emotion wants us to do: understand the signal before we pivot toward goal-oriented action.

First, we need to look at our goals. Imagine we are at a work meeting, and our boss makes what we believe to be a demeaning comment about our creative problem-solving skills. It's easy to focus on her words rather than examine the situation and the goals more broadly. We may see multiple goals active in us at the moment. We, of course, want to keep our job. And we also want to feel valued and respected for our creativity. After some self-reflection, we may discover that one of our goals (which is often implicit) is to seem smarter than everyone else. We may want to show off our creative talents and have people admire us. Here we need to make some choices—about which of the wants are core and integral to who we are and our development and which are peripheral wants, symptomatic of unfulfilled central wants. We need to re-choose our goals wisely.

Then, we can reflect on our cognitive constructs or beliefs. Are they informed and accurate? Is my belief that my boss used a mocking tone aligned with what I know to be true from our previous history and experience? Could the lens through which I view my boss be systemically distorted by my past experiences of bullying at work, or even as a child?

4. We strategize. Once we are satisfied with our goals and constructs, it's important not to plunge into hasty action without understanding the subtleties of the situation. When in the midst of strong negative emotions, we are frequently fixated on the threats and obstacles rather than refocused on what we want.

We may realize one of our wants is to feel respected and valued in our workplace. This is not the same as wanting our boss to respect us (which is peripheral, given our boss's feelings are not under our control). To reach our want, we need to strategize, and this may take various prongs: reassessment of our own values and work style as well as that of the organizational culture we are embedded in. What is under our control is finding better ways of contributing value to our workplace, better communication strategies with our boss, and if that doesn't improve the situation, finding another boss or job.

5. We create an action plan and act on it. We can strategize all we want, but if we don't create and implement an action plan, the emotion will keep sending its message. Once we start acting, the negative emotion will likely diminish in intensity until it disappears. The emotion has done its job. The friend leaves our house and returns only when new troubles or challenges arrive.

Now that we know how to employ choice when negative emotions arrive, we could also ask ourselves if there are practices that we can employ long term to help us cultivate our resilience. Resilience allows us to not just cope but flourish in uncertain and troubling circumstances.

Long-Term Tools for Resilience

We cultivate resilience by applying the lever of choice to all components of our emotions. If we look at Figure 4.4, we'll see all the places we can apply choice: to wants, situations, constructs or beliefs, and expression of emotions through action.

1. We can apply choice on which *wants* or *goals* we want to pursue. As humans, we are not constrained by the survival and reproduction goals that are the evolutionary heritage of nonhuman mammals. We have many unique core wants. The more we choose

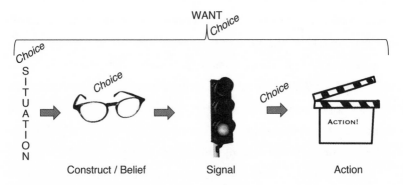

FIGURE 4.4 Choice Points for Building Resilience

developmental (rather than peripheral) wants, the more we will have emotions about things that are under our control, rather than under the control of other people or the world.

When Aisha wanted a promotion (which depended not just on her performance but on the opinions and prejudices of others around her) she set the stage for many months of negative emotions since she couldn't control what others thought about her. When she regrouped and realized that her developmental want was having self-worth and contributing confidently to her work, she had a plan of action. Even when it didn't work well and she experienced temporary negative emotions that come from setbacks, she could regroup, strategize, and continue to pursue her wants. *Focusing on developmental wants that we can do something about means that other people don't control our emotions; we do.*

Furthermore, humans feel emotion not just in relation to reality (what is in front of us), as all apes do, but also in relation to our imagination (future) and memory (past). Abhinav felt so much guilt about how much his parents suffered years ago that it prevented him from making healthy choices for his own life in the present. We can all remember the times we have been hurt, betrayed, or experienced a loss and feel all these old emotions again and again. While anticipating future threats is a great tool that helps us to avoid danger, our minds can also spin many future fears which are not entirely under our control (are we going to destroy the planet, will we get Alzheimer's disease, will our loved ones die before we do, and so on). If we don't find something we can *do* about future or past events, the negative emotions may keep running on a loop. *Having negative emotions about things that are before us, and that we can do something about, is the best use of our emotional system.*

2. **We can apply choice to the *situations* we choose to put ourselves in and how to change our environment to suit us better.**

Unlike nonhuman mammals, we are not at the mercy of our environment. We can shape our world and choose the situations we enter. If we are an elderly person with limited mobility and live in a house that no longer works for us (lots of stairs, slippery surfaces, a deep tub, etc.), change is possible. Whether that means moving entirely to the ground floor of the house, installing aids to mobility, getting helpers to prevent injury, or even moving to a more easily navigable living space, these are choices that can change our environment so it doesn't cause constant negative emotion (fear, anger, sadness) or injury.

Furthermore, we can choose which situations we enter so that they don't overwhelm us with negative emotions. For example, we may not mind being a little afraid of a new, more challenging job. On the other hand, we may hold back from leaving our job entirely to pursue our own start-up, given how much fear this new situation would give us. *As humans, we can gauge which situations we want to enter, and which circumstances we want to change, to optimize our emotional life.*

3. We can apply our choice to change the *beliefs or constructs* through which we see the world. Thinking of ourselves as works in progress rather than failures will determine whether we feel self-compassion or shame. Seeing a new project as a challenge rather than a burden will make us either excited or frustrated when we work on it. Thinking of the natural world as doomed to destruction rather than worthy of protecting will leave us either hopeless or energized. In the end, we need to choose which constructs *work* best, that is, lead us to fulfillment of our wants.

Sometimes, we can have multiple constructs through which we see the situation and we can choose among them. Let's say a colleague passes by us without responding to our greeting. If we have a construct that she is a rude person, we will be angry; if we have a construct that she is preoccupied with some trouble we don't know about, we may become compassionate; if we believe she is angry and didn't say hello on purpose, we may be afraid; and if we have a construct that she probably didn't see us, we may not feel any emotion at all. Given that most of the time we don't have enough information, this multitude of constructs can encourage us to collect more information (such as by reaching out to the colleague). Then we can check what was the most accurate assessment of the situation and update our construct to be more accurate.

4. We can apply choice to whether and how to *express emotion through action* when it arrives. When the negative emotion arrives, we can make a choice to turn the PFC switch to the on position so we can strategize how to reach our long-term goals. We can choose *whether* to express the emotion, *when* to express it, and *how* to express it.

Notice that emotion *expression* (playing out the emotion-appropriate energy signature) is not the same as *processing* (receiving and acting on the message emotion is sending). As we saw before with anger and fear, fully automatic expression of emotion through action (with PFC in the off position) will have us tackling colleagues to the ground, yelling at border officials, and rear-ending every car that cuts us off in traffic. We know from experience that someone yelling at others in anger doesn't run out of anger. Counterintuitively, research shows expressions of anger increase, rather than decrease, anger and subsequent aggression.[6] In humans, emotion expression and processing are independent as long as we are not actively suppressing emotions.

The "cathartic" model, which is supposed to make the sadness go away after a good cry, or anger after we have done some verbal punching at our target, unfortunately, may even lead to emotions' prolonged stay. The reason is that only expressing our emotions doesn't require us to interpret the message the emotion is sending us or do what emotion wants us to do—move closer to our goals. This is not to say that we should not express our emotions (if it doesn't hurt us or others) since, for some of us, the expression is our first clue that we are experiencing an emotion. However, it's worthwhile to remember that while the expression will dissipate some of the active energy our bodies inherited from our evolutionary history, after the expression, we will still be left with a processing job to do. Over the long term, we can cultivate what type and level of expression works best for us and helps us process our emotions most effectively.

When our emotional system is working well, we can move past our obstacles and threats toward our wants and pivot from our losses toward reengagement with new goals and relationships. The practice of processing negative emotions gives us trust that we can handle and deal with them the next time they arrive. But what happens when the emotion doesn't leave, when we continue being sad, resentful, guilty, or ashamed, sometimes for years? Now we turn to sticky emotions that can't just be processed but need to be "**reprocessed.**"

STICKY EMOTIONS

What happens if emotions don't leave us but stick around? Continuing to experience the same emotion no matter the circumstance over extended periods of time may be a sign that *the construct or lens we are using to look at the situations is distorted or "closed."* In the chapter on motivation, we talked about how constructs are supposed to be continually updated with new information. Their continual change based on life experiences is what makes them informative. But if they stop being updated, if they "close" at some point in our lives, they stop being helpful in understanding ourselves and those around us.

If the construct through which we view the world is closed, *it will always give us the same answer; that is, the same emotion* (Figure 4.5).

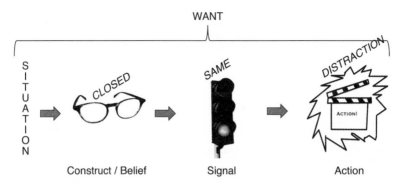

FIGURE 4.5   Sticky Emotions

If you have the closed construct "People can't be trusted," then fear and disappointment are likely to mark all your relationships—at work, with friends, and with family. The construct "I'm not good enough" may cause constant shame, sadness, or regret. Parts of our lives that have stalled are often marked by the closed constructs which lead to sticky emotions that don't go away.

While in parts of our lives that are going well, emotions signal something about the world (dangers, obstacles, losses, etc.), in stalled parts of our lives the sticky emotions signal that there is something distorted about our constructs. While healthy emotion goes away once we do something in relation to the world (protect ourselves or realign ourselves with our goals), *sticky emotions can leave only once we change our closed constructs, reopening them to reality. In short, we need to act on ourselves.*

To do that we need to **reprocess** our emotions, which includes first finding sticky emotions and then discovering the closed constructs that are triggering them. If we feel shame all the time because of the construct "I'll always be a failure," no amount of external success will help us not feel the continual shame. For shame to go away, we need to act on the construct itself.

Anything that we experience for a prolonged period can fade into the background of our life, and the same is the case with emotions. If our emotions are negative, we often try to avoid, suppress, or distract ourselves from them. Given that we want to rediscover our sticky emotions to reprocess them, how are we to do that?

One thing we may do is give ourselves some periods of silence and quiet. For many of us who have stalled in some aspects of our development, being silently present with ourselves without physical or mental interaction can be an aversive experience. If caught accidentally in a quiet moment (let's say, sitting in a car during rush hour, folding laundry, or waiting in line at a grocery store), we would try to change the situation. We would turn on the radio, look at our phone, think about our to-do list, read the news, scroll through social media, or try to engage with the world. Avoiding silence is a rational response to the fear of negative emotions that tends to emerge in that silent space. Emotions we feel in quiet are markers of what kind of relationship we have with ourselves. One way to bring the sticky emotions to the forefront of our experience would be to give ourselves a period of silence and watch what emotions show up.

Another thing we do to cover up sticky emotions is to fill the silent space with **distractions or overdoing** that move our attention away from the negative emotions or **addictions** that give us substitutive comfort we talked about in Chapter Two. Often the clues to what upsets us the most come from watching what precedes the action of turning on the TV or reaching for the cigarette or ice cream.

In our everyday experience, we usually go from our situation (let's say silence) to a construct ("I'm not good enough"), to emotion (shame), to a distraction (reaching for our phone) within seconds (Figure 4.6). If we want to **reprocess** our sticky emotions (first find them, and then figure out which closed construct caused them), we need to work a bit backward.

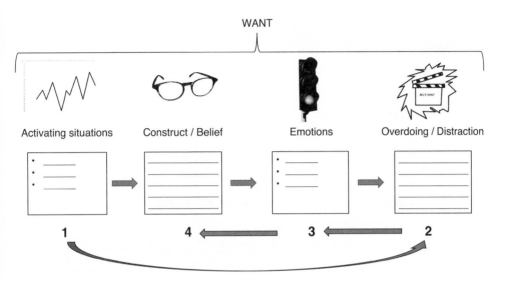

FIGURE 4.6   Stages of Reprocessing Emotion

Let's start with a triggering situation (marked 1 in Figure 4.6), which within seconds sends us to distraction (marked 2). Just as we are about to reach for the ice cream, cigarette, or scroll through our social media feed, we can stop ourselves and ask the following: What will I feel if I don't do this? Will I feel restless, dissatisfied, anxious, ashamed, angry, or bored? This will help us find the sticky emotions we are trying not to feel (box marked 3).

For Emily, it was the silence (situation) that compelled her to fill all the empty crevices of the day by checking on how her investments were performing (distraction). When she stopped doing it, she felt dissatisfied and restless (emotion).

For Aisha, it was as simple as seeing a colleague who was promoted instead of her (situation) that would send her to her LinkedIn feed (distraction). When she would prevent herself from checking LinkedIn, she realized she was feeling anger, anxiety, and envy, all at the same time (emotion).

Kai would get upset whenever he had to interact with his own body—changing clothes or exercising (situation)—which made him want to eat more or play video games (distraction). If he was stuck somewhere (like on a beach) where he couldn't easily get to his distractors, he'd feel shame (emotion).

Finally, Abhinav would get activated whenever there was more work that he didn't want to take on but also couldn't turn down. He would try not to think about it—watching TV or scrolling his social media feeds (distraction). Saying no usually would send him into a deep feeling of guilt (emotion).

There is one last step (marked 4 in Figure 4.6) and that is guessing which closed constructs are causing our sticky emotions. Though we will go deeply into discussing constructs in Chapter Five, in Technique 3 you will be asked to give your best guess of what your closed constructs are. At this stage, you can think of them simply as thoughts that pop up in your mind just before you start feeling the sticky emotion. In the next sections, you will see how each of our protagonists explored their own constructs. Then you will be asked to try reprocessing emotions yourselves.

Persistent Guilt

Healthy guilt lets us know that we made a mistake in a relationship. It requires us to acknowledge and, if possible, repair the damage we caused, never to make a similar mistake again. We'll feel guilty if we knock off another car's side mirror in the parking lot, and then try to escape the responsibility. Guilt should lead us to leave a note under the windshield of the damaged car with our contact information. Or if it comes too late, to acknowledge what happened, and make sure we know what we should do the next time around. But what if we have guilt that doesn't go away?

Let's look at Abhinav, who identified guilt as one of his sticky emotions. If he was thinking about declining a patient who wanted help and at the same time prevented himself from distracting, he felt overpowering guilt. He then asked himself, "What thoughts pop up in my mind just before I feel guilty?" The answer surprised him. The thoughts that showed up were not about the patients but his parents. He thought, "I should have helped them more."

What Abhinav was referring to is that when he was young, his parents worked multiple jobs and sacrificed greatly to make sure he and his brother got a good education. Like all other kids, Abhinav would occasionally goof off and play with his brother rather than study and help around the house. Whenever he was about to turn down more work, his parents' sacrifices would show up in his mind and he would experience deep guilt.

Although Abhinav helped his parents tremendously over the years, these guilt-causing thoughts would come again and again. He was having emotions about events in the past, driven by a closed construct that was frozen in time. Once he started putting his thoughts down on paper, he noticed other thoughts showed up too: "They suffered so much to get me my education, I should suffer in my work too," and "Knowing that I work this hard will make them think their sacrifices were worth it." These constructs were also closed—they had stayed the same since Abhinav's childhood. Notice the constructs causing persistent emotion are not about what is before us but what is behind us, and that they are frozen in time, untouched by what happened since the events.

The realistic, or open, construct would be more updated: "I didn't help them much as a kid, and I regret the times I didn't do my chores, but since I've grown up, I've been making sure I do my part and that they have everything they need. I'll continue to do that since I want them to feel loved and appreciated." Without opening the closed construct, we can't move beyond our sticky emotions.

Persistent Regret

Regret is perhaps the most recognizable of the sticky emotions, which many seem to carry to their graves. Yet regret, like all other emotions, has evolved as a temporary signal for us to learn that we could have benefited from a different path at a particular juncture in our life. While guilt deals with mistakes we have made that hurt others, regret often includes the hurt we have inflicted on ourselves too. Whether it's regretting not starting a business we would be passionate about or having an affair that had cost us a marriage, both actions and inactions of the past are something we can learn from. Our regret is supposed to orient us to not repeat our mistakes, to bring what we want into our life (entrepreneurship), and leave out what we don't (affairs). So, what happens when regrets last?

Emily had made a career choice early in her life, based on the following constructs that were passed on to her by her father: "You can work on your art only once you are financially secure" and "Either you become a success at what you do or better not try." It had set her on a path that made her very successful but also deeply dissatisfied and without a creative outlet in her life. Whenever a space of quiet would open in her day, a thought ("Maybe I should have tried being an artist") would sneak into her mind, making her restless and regretful. But she'd quickly pivot back to her current construct—that she was successful and that she had made the right decision to follow her path. But the other option, the path not taken, kept sneaking up on her and disturbing her peace.

Notice how constructs that include "should" in them are aspirational statements. In Emily's case, it was how the younger self should have been. So many of us have this experience: "If I only had done X in my past, my whole life would be different." *Yet all of us make the best decisions we can, given the developmental stage we are at.* Aspirational constructs about our past selves like the company of other similar constructs (such as "I should have known better," "I should have been more developed by that age," and so on.) This shows a lack of compassion for the self and a lack of understanding of how development functions (forward, not backward). Furthermore, there is no way to know how a different decision would have played out in our lives. All we have is the present, which is where we can make choices, wisely remembering our potential past mistakes.

An open and more updated construct for Emily may look something like, "I can do art a little or a lot, with or without being financially secure." Regrets require learning what we can from the past to enrich our present. We don't learn from blaming ourselves backward in time for not being developed enough. If we do that, it's understandable why regrets never leave us.

Resentment

Let us look at a different emotion that also has a reputation for sticking around. Anger, when processed, allows us to get closer to our goals by overcoming obstacles life throws our way. How is resentment different?

While trying to advance in her career, Aisha noticed how being a woman of color had hurt her path to promotion. Less qualified and talented engineers had been promoted past her, while she was left behind and asked to "upskill" and develop leadership skills or more executive "presence." When she examined thoughts that occurred just before strong resentment would arise in her, she realized the construct that kept recurring was "The world should be just," or "I should be respected."

She noticed that all the statements that would show up in her mind had this aspirational, or "should," form. When seen as aspirations, these statements are admirable, particularly when they activate us to make the world more just. But when used as constructs that reflect reality (which clearly contradicts it), it leads to a situation that is impossible to resolve.

A realistic construct for Aisha may look like this: "The world is often unjust and can be made more just through action to overcome structural prejudice." If that was her construct, Aisha could feel anger and orient her action to do what's within her control given the prejudice and unfairness that surrounded her. But with an aspiration, rather than reality, stuck in a place of a construct, she was left simmering with resentment and escalating behaviors she thought would get her the job if the world were indeed just—working harder and leading more projects.

In resentment, we act on the world as if our aspirational constructs were true and keep receiving a resounding "no" back from the world. Accepting reality in the moment (the fact of current injustice, racism, or prejudice) doesn't mean we can't act on it to be different in the future. But our constructs need to accurately represent reality, and not our hopes, if we are ever to have a chance of making the difference we wish for.

Persistent Shame

While healthy shame lets us know we have behaved in a way that deeply misaligns with who we aspire to be and offers a corrective path, persistent shame is different. It seems to signal to us that we are bad and terrible at our very core, and the action it seems to cause in us is to make us want to disappear. What is very destructive about persistent shame is that constructs such as "I am terrible," "I am rotten," and "I am disgusting" seem to come spontaneously to us, as if they were a part of us. Yet knowing what we know about emotions should put us on high alert that something strange is going on. Why would emotions signal to us that we are terrible rather than guide us toward our goals?

Let's go back to Kai, and remember he noted shame was one of his central emotions. Although Kai said he felt comfortable being himself most of the time, some situations would cause him to experience sudden shame. If he was at the beach or pool, he would try to stay in shorts and a T-shirt and would be overcome by a feeling of shame because of his body. He felt everyone around him was disgusted, and he would try to leave the situation as quickly as he could, no matter how much his friends would try to convince him to stay.

The key thing to remember with persistent shame is that the constructs that appear, seemingly ready made, in our mind—"I am disgusting," or "I am terrible"—did not originate in our own mind. Toddlers need to be taught how to relate to themselves, including what to think of their bodies. The construct "My body is disgusting" had to come from somewhere—whether from caregivers, other kids, relatives, or the media. In Kai's case, it was his father, who was a runner and very fastidious about his own weight, who brought the construct into Kai's mind. It wasn't necessarily what he said but a series of experiences: Disgust on his father's face when he saw him changing clothes; having his father take food off his plate and forcing him to go running early in the morning.

The problem with persistent shame is that when our mind tricks us into believing these constructs are our own and are realistic appraisals of who we are, there is nothing left to do but feel shame and try not to be visible. These closed constructs displace any realistic beliefs we may have of ourselves and prevent us from knowing ourselves and growing. This is why it's so important to identify experiences of persistent shame and the underlying constructs that feed the relentless pain it brings us.

Now that we have observed four different sticky emotions, we may notice a pattern. They seem to be driven by constructs that don't represent reality (of ourselves, others, or the world) and have been closed to information a long time ago.

Now it's your turn to try to identify your own sticky emotions and closed constructs as you practice reprocessing emotion.

TECHNIQUE 3: REPROCESSING EMOTIONS

You are now at the midpoint of getting the Wheel of Self moving again. After having rediscovered your central wants and restored enough willpower to intervene in your inner self, it's time to work on emotions. Figure 4.7 will help you uncover sticky emotions in the domain of your life that feels stalled and guide you to investigate constructs that may be contributing to the persistent and intrusive negative emotions. Below are step-by-step instructions and an illustrative example.

STEP 1: *Write down what situations activate or "trigger" strong negative emotions in the domain of your want. They will be the situations that will make you reach for your distractors. Notice situations you avoid, that make you strongly uncomfortable, or that make you think about your past failed attempts to gain what you desire. You can review your work on Technique 1 to stimulate thinking about what activates you.*

Example: Imagine that we have tried to become financially successful, for years, without achieving it. Given that finances are the

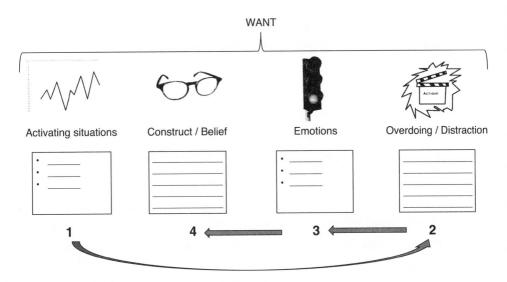

FIGURE 4.7 Technique 3: Reprocessing Emotion

domain of our desire, we get activated whenever we see someone displaying wealth (expensive cars, watches, clothes), when we look at our own bank account, when we are at a restaurant and can't order expensive things on the menu, or whenever the topic of investments comes up with friends. To avoid being activated, we may avoid going out to restaurants or malls and may even avoid looking at our own bank account.

Any circumstance that gives you an emotion that is much stronger than the situation warrants is likely to be an activating one. We often call these responses "overreactions." If you are having a minor disagreement with a friend over which restaurant you should pick for dinner, getting upset and yelling at them could be considered to be an overreaction. Burning your rice on the stove and breaking down in tears over it is another example of overreaction. The reaction is logical and "properly sized" but the cause is usually invisible to those outside us. In the case of yelling at our friend, what we are angry at is not them but our inability to afford any of the restaurants we are discussing. In the case of burnt rice, we are not sad about rice but at our inability to see ourselves as competent. Try to think what kind of situations cause overreactions in you.

STEP 2: *Place your overdoing activities and distractors you worked on in the box marked 2. Notice that you will already have your list ready from working through Technique 2. If additional things come up, feel free to add them. What are all the ways you try to avoid feeling sticky emotions?*

Example: Whenever activated by others' financial success, we try to distract ourselves by working out or talking to our partner because it makes us feel better. Another thing we may do is "overdo"—start reading investment advice blogs and articles, make new and more extreme monthly budgets, and so forth. Everything that we do to avoid "sitting with" the experience of the negative emotion belongs here. Notice that even seemingly healthy behaviors (such as exercise) can act as distractors when used to not feel a sticky emotion.

STEP 3: *What emotions do you feel just before you distract/overdo? These are the negative emotions that are always in the background and that seep out if we take a pause or don't manage to properly distract ourselves. Just before your distractor, take a pause and try to experience the emotion that is coming up for you. If you are not sure what emotion you are feeling, feel free to notice anything you are experiencing in the moment—like "feel numb," "feel bad," or "feel my heart racing."*

Example: Being activated by other people's financial success and not being able to distract ourselves, we would feel envy, hopelessness, and shame about our financial situation.

STEP 4: *Take each emotion from the list in the box marked 3, and ask yourself what thoughts come up just before (or as) this emotion emerges.*

Write as many thoughts as possible that come up for you. Then move on to the second emotion, and third, depending on how many you have. There is no right number of constructs that you need for each emotion. It can be one or ten, depending on your experience.

Example: We could start with envy and realize what comes up in our mind is "I am smarter than they are, so I should have more money than they do." When unpacking shame, different thoughts may come up, such as "What kind of a person is not financially secure by my age?" or "I'm good for nothing," or "I'll always be a failure."

You may be wondering whether you are writing down the "right" thoughts. What if they are not the closed constructs that we talked about in the previous sections but just simply thoughts that pop up in your mind? How would you be able to tell the difference? At this point, try not to overthink this process. If you have a thought that makes you feel bad (in any way) or makes you want to overdo or distract, just write it down. In the next chapter, we'll get a lot of practice recognizing what makes a construct closed or "frozen." For now, write down anything that comes to mind.

Once you have completed Technique 3, you'll know what sticky emotions lead you to distraction and overdoing and what constructs or beliefs are likely feeding these emotions. Now it's time to turn to our next topic—how to sift through all the thoughts that pop up in our mind, how to recognize closed constructs, and finally, how to prepare to reopen them to reality.

CHAPTER FIVE

MIND

We have now reached the part of our inner work in which we have to reflect on constructs and beliefs that contribute to our inability to get what we desire the most. When a closed construct (such as "I'm not good enough to get promoted") shows up in Aisha's mind, along with other thoughts (such as "I'm good at math" or "Working hard will get me a promotion"), how is she supposed to recognize which ones are accurate and which ones distorted?

When constructs or beliefs show up in our minds, it's difficult not to believe them. What creates them? What makes them "pop up"? How are we to challenge some of our thoughts without challenging all of them? To answer these questions, we need to understand how the mind works, how thoughts show up, and how to recognize and understand constructs that are closed to information and therefore static and unreliable.

THREE MINDS

It is far more difficult to get to the truth of ourselves by using our minds than we commonly believe. Like a well-trained lawyer, the mind can argue any side of a case. And when our Wheel of Self is stalled because some of our constructs are frozen in time and don't reflect the reality of ourselves or the world, it is this same mind we need to use to get it moving again.

The mind, in fact, is the central lever that can notice the problem in the self and apply techniques and experiences that will guide it toward change. That's exactly what we do, for example, when we use our mind to probe our wants, understand rather than distract from strong negative emotions, and intervene to reshape parts of our nervous system to lay down new neural pathways. We will learn how to best use the mind by knowing more about it.

How can the mind do such contradictory things—be the cause of the problems and the pathway to its solution? How can the mind intervene in the mind? It does so by not being one mind. Instead of thinking of ourselves as having one mind, we can think of having three: (1) the Problem Solver (the conscious mind), (2) the Intuiter (the unconscious mind), and (3) the Choice-Maker (the metamind). Each of these minds has its own unique qualities and its own blind spots. We should acquaint ourselves with all three to use each to the best of their potential.

The Problem Solver (Conscious Mind)

Imagine yourself at a restaurant. You've just had a great meal with your partner. It's getting late in the evening, and you ask for your bill. The server gives it to you but apologizes that the card machine is not working, and you'll have to pay by cash. You take out your wallet and, looking at the bill, start to calculate the 18 percent tip in your mind. Your partner starts to say something but stops—you are clearly not listening as you make the calculation in your mind. You find that even the music in the restaurant, which you barely noticed up to this point, is now distracting. But you manage to block it all out, and after some short and painful mental gymnastics, you are done. You pay the bill and relax into the post-dinner conversation.

What has just happened? For a few seconds, while calculating the tip, you turned on your conscious mind, the Problem Solver. This is the mind we most identify with—the one that can do complex calculations, think through a difficult problem, and carve a path toward a solution. This mind, which we believe does everything for us, turns out to be a very small, powerful, and energy-expensive imagining device. It is small in terms of both how many things we can have in our minds at the same time and how quickly it processes information. Figure 5.1 shows a summary of its qualities.

According to most recent research, we can comfortably hold three to five things in our mind at the same time.[1] The real question then becomes what we mean by a "thing." A phone number may have 10 digits, but we still can remember it because we can "chunk" the area code into one "thing." People living in Toronto, for example, don't remember numbers four, one, and six as three different

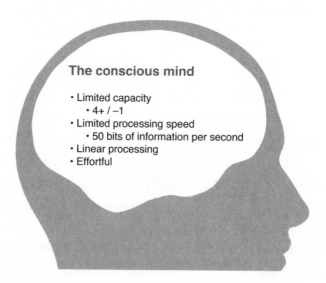

The conscious mind

- Limited capacity
  - 4+ / −1
- Limited processing speed
  - 50 bits of information per second
- Linear processing
- Effortful

FIGURE 5.1   Qualities of the Problem Solver Mind

chunks. It's a 416 area code, and therefore, only one chunk in their mind. We can easily make a pattern out of a string of random digits and make them into a chunk. Experts can hold more information in their minds than novices because their knowledge of the subject matter makes them more skilled at packaging more complex patterns into one chunk.[2] Imagine what a chess master can hold in her mind compared with a chess novice, who can barely remember how each piece moves.

In terms of processing speed, we seem to be able to process about 50 bits of information each second (which corresponds to reading one short sentence of about five words per second).[3] This makes sense, given that the conscious mind is a linear processor and able to process time well. Temporal awareness (of "before" or "after") makes language possible. For example, we construct sentences by stringing sequences of words in time. Awareness of time also allows people to view themselves temporally in terms of past experiences and future goals and construct an identity for themselves.

The linearity of conscious processing is also what makes multitasking (that is, simultaneity) of two mentally complex tasks that require a conscious mind impossible for most of us. Usually, effective multitasking involves one conscious task (like discussing a difficult issue with a friend over the phone) and one or more automatic tasks that don't require conscious attention (driving a car or folding laundry). Multitasking two tasks for which we require a conscious mind would be like writing a demanding email while simultaneously having a difficult phone conversation on a different topic. For most of us, it would result in an error in either task (or both). Also, when a task that is usually automatic (like driving) becomes cognitively demanding—such as when we get lost or hit an ice patch—to reduce our mental load, we are likely to turn off the radio or stop talking to other people in the car. Multitasking, therefore, is best done as a collaboration between the conscious and unconscious mind (or mentally complex and automatized processes).

Despite its linearity and apparent slowness, conscious thinking shaped us into the unique species we are. The beauty of the conscious mind is its calculating and imagining capacity. It has landed humans on the moon, made experiments bringing us lifesaving vaccines, and cracked codes for long-extinct languages. In addition to the capacity to manipulate symbols, the conscious mind's simulating capacity has also enabled us to transform human relationships to create complex networks of interpersonal connections. The Problem Solver is the key to our continuing to explore the hidden treasures in the sciences and the arts.

However, thinking is an effortful, time-consuming process, as we can tell by how we feel after we have finished doing our taxes. Very few people feel refreshed by bouts of effortful and sustained thinking. (The effortless process of having thoughts will be described in the next section.) The effort involved in conscious thinking combined with its small processing speed highlights that it would not be well suited for processing enormous amounts of information coming to us every day. Rather, if conscious processing (or thinking) were how we dealt with all the information coming from the world (such as those processed by the five senses) as well as from our internal functions (digesting food, moving our body, or breathing), we would not last long as species. There is simply too much information that we process every day, internally and externally, for the Problem Solver to digest. Everything essential to our survival seems to have evolved to be dealt with by the other mind—the unconscious mind, which all animals have.

The Intuiter (Unconscious Mind)

If you take a Sunday-morning walk and take in the sounds of the city; feel the morning breeze; see trees, stores, and people walking by; and smell the coffee from the cup you carry in your hand—this flurry of sensory information is effortlessly and almost instantaneously organized into a coherent sensory experience. If you meet a friend and he asks if the bookshop you had passed on the way to his house was open, you may be able to recall that it was, although when you were passing it, you weren't paying it any particular attention. It means you can often recall or act on the information you collected unconsciously. It remains dormant unless you need to act on it.

The mind that was doing all the work while you were enjoying your morning stroll is the Intuiter—the unconscious mind. This mind has seemingly unlimited capacity; that is, the limit is unknown to us. At no point in our old age, even when our sensory organs (such as ears and eyes) start failing us, does the brain place a firm limit on sensory information and refuse to process it. Given its immense capacity, the unconscious is where we store all our learnings, including our expertise.

In terms of processing speed, the most conservative accounts put it at 11 million bits per second, a staggeringly fast system enabled by parallel synaptic processing, a hallmark of our nervous system.[4] Compared with the conscious mind (and its 50 bits per second), the unconscious mind processes a staggeringly vaster amount of information every second of the day. We can see a summary of its qualities in Figure 5.2.

The unconscious mind turns out to be a huge, fast data processor, and what we call an instinct is a thought, emotion, or urge to action that is the result of all the processing done by the unconscious mind. This is also where all that we have learned in our life waits patiently until we need it, and then just "shows up" in our awareness. When we look at our closest animal relatives, apes, they seem to be able to do a very complex set of functions, including defending territory, mating, and nurturing their young, without having what we consider a human-like conscious mind.

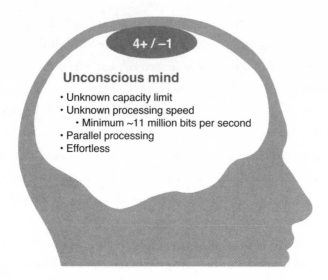

FIGURE 5.2 Qualities of the Intuiter Mind

Most of us, in fact, can spend large parts of our days functioning very well without turning on the conscious mind and actively thinking. Not only is most of our mental processing unconscious but most of the goals that guide us to everyday activities are also embedded in this unconscious network.[5] For example, all the wants we have been exploring with Technique 1 were embedded in our unconscious mind and acting on us continually without us necessarily knowing what they were.

Furthermore, most of the thoughts we experience in our minds are not the ones we have "thought up" by our conscious mind but those that simply "pop up" from the unconscious mind. Unlike the conscious activity *inside* the awareness, in which we actively **think**, here we **have thoughts**—passively and effortlessly receive them in our awareness. Why is this important? Because the closed constructs that our protagonists have been struggling with—Abhinav's "I should have helped them more" or Aisha's "Maybe I don't deserve the promotion"—came to their awareness automatically from their un-conscious mind. Since they show up ready-made with all the other beliefs, it means that we'd need to develop a special technique (which we'll discuss at the end of the chapter) to identify them as closed and reopen them to new, more accurate, information.

Just as the unconscious can be a source of problems, it can bring us solutions. While we sleep and our conscious processing has been turned off for the night, the unconscious mind continues associat-ing and surfacing images, thoughts, and actions in our dreams. A very important stage of the creative process, incubation, is done in an exclusively unconscious way, and many scientists have claimed to have found clues to the scientific or mathematical problems that have long evaded them in their dreams.[6]

It's important to remember that the unconscious has as much cre-ative power as the thinking mind. Although all the "ingredients" that the nervous system works with are old (in the sense that they are made of our past sensations, thoughts, knowledge, etc.), these vast stores of information can be combined in the unconscious space in creative, even genius ways. The idea can be a remarkable break-through by the time it pops up in our heads. The cartoonish moment of a lightbulb turning on above our heads symbolizes one of these ideas springing from the unconscious.

The effortlessness of the Intuiter is very appealing, given how much energy the Problem Solver spends. Walking down the street, seeing the world, or interacting with people doesn't seem particularly effortful unless we encounter a problem that requires conscious pro-cessing. Even when doing an exclusively cognitive activity, such as sitting in a classroom and listening to an interesting lecture, we are still likely to mostly be *having thoughts*. While there may appear to be many things happening in our minds—we are comprehending sentences, free-associating with what we hear, taking notes, and having creative thoughts emerge in our mind—all this mental activity is effortless, and we may leave the lecture even more energized than when we entered it. We can have many thoughts, sensations, and experiences and reshape our cognitive world in interesting and fresh ways without ever having to think. This does not mean we will not have learned or not had many creative thoughts about the lecture. It only means that the work has been done effortlessly, by our unconscious system.

If we only had the Problem Solver and the Intuiter as our minds, we could never challenge what they say. Kai's closed construct "I am disgusting" would stay with him forever. Aisha's mistaken calculations of what will gain her the promotion would never be corrected. Fortunately, there is a third mind that observes what the Problem Solver and the Intuiter are up to. But who, or what, inside of us could be observing both thinking and having thoughts?

The Choice-Maker (Metamind)

Imagine you are being interviewed at a company you very much want to work in. It took a considerable effort to get the interview, you have prepared well, and now you are hoping you can ace it. It starts off well and the interviewer seems friendly. However, about halfway through the interview, you get this question: "What do you think are challenges our company will encounter due to the competitor expansion over the next three years?" Even though you thought you prepared well, you haven't researched their competitors at all. And as your Problem Solver is frantically searching your mind for any clues as to how to answer the question and the Intuiter stays stubbornly silent, you can see that the interview is about to crumble. You have only a confused jumble of thoughts in your mind, and as you are watching it, you know you won't find an answer, let alone a good one.

What has just happened? Who is watching the Problem Solver and Intuiter in action? We often assume it's the Problem Solver doing the observing, placing the conscious mind in a strange position of solving a complex problem and watching itself at the same time. Being able to watch ourselves think and have thoughts points to the presence of another mind, the Choice-Maker. Without it, we wouldn't be capable of metacognition—we couldn't think about thinking or having thoughts.

When things are going well, the metamind can inconspicuously direct attention to whatever is relevant at the moment. For example, we can move our attention to the clicks that the keyboard makes as we are typing, to what is happening on the screen in front of us, to thoughts that the Intuiter "popped up" into awareness, or to the behavioral impulse to go to the kitchen and refill our coffee cup. We can direct this "flashlight" of attention to yesterday, to ten years ago, to an imagination of what we believe next month's weather will be like, or to a complex mathematical task. If our interview is going well, we can be effortlessly mindful of the interviewer's facial expressions, the environment, relevant questions, and so forth.

If there's a problem, as in the interview example, the metamind directs attention to what it believes to be the source of the problem— our own mind. We become *self-conscious*. If you are the interviewee, your flashlight of attention would turn to the disturbed expression on the interviewer's face, your own sweaty palms, and the confused thoughts you are thinking up in your head. Your Choice-Maker would also make a decision. Do you fake your way through an incoherent answer, do you smile and acknowledge that you haven't done research on their competitors and hope they don't take it against you, or do you give up and walk out? Whenever the metamind activates (whether while we struggle to give a presentation or are the first person on the dance floor), self-consciousness indicates that the Choice-Maker has noticed that something may be amiss and has directed itself to our own mind and body.

The Choice-Maker not only directs the flashlight of attention but also makes decisions. It can change what data we consume, what we consider important, and what we decide not to think about. It can notice (or decide not to) what thoughts surface from the unconscious mind. Whereas the Problem Solver is bound to process whatever the Intuiter surfaces (information often dictated by our past learnings and patterns), the Choice-Maker can interrupt old patterns and build new ways of thinking, feeling, desiring, and behaving. Without a metamind, all of us would be at the mercy of our circumstances, forced to replay our old patterns for as long as we live.

Given that our Choice-Maker is monitoring our two minds for signs of trouble, how is it that we end up with closed constructs, which don't reflect reality and lead us to get stalled in some domain of our life? There are two reasons. First, the Choice-Maker can occasionally fall asleep and let go of the flashlight. This is when we are mindless, on autopilot. [7] When that happens, the flashlight is taken up by the Intuiter—who shines it on what will move us in the direction of our unconscious wants and sees the world through constructs it has at its disposal. For example, if our Choice-Maker falls asleep while we are mindlessly scrolling through our social media feed, we can reach for and eat unhealthy snacks on "autopilot," without noticing it happened.

Even when we are fully in charge of the flashlight of attention, we may choose to keep shining it on others, and the world, rather than turn it back on ourselves. To detect and update our closed constructs, the Choice-Maker has to turn its attention back to the two minds, and that can be unpleasant and tiring. Emily, for example, was very focused and in charge of what she paid attention to (her professional tasks), yet she was still dissatisfied and unfulfilled. What she wasn't doing was directing her attention to the source of her problem—exploring why she believed we need to have a lot of money to have the freedom to be creative. She was simply acting as if the belief were true. Without directing the Choice-Maker to illuminate our own closed constructs, we are likely to not get what we want, over and over again.

SHOULD WE BELIEVE OUR THOUGHTS?

Now that we know our three minds, we can ask if any of them are more likely to take us closer to the truth of ourselves, others, or the world. Should we mistrust the Intuiter since its data selection and processing are occluded from our sight? Should we disbelieve the Problem Solver, given its limited storage space and processing power? Should the Choice-Maker be the final arbiter of the truth, or is it too often missing in action to be relied upon? Answering this question of who or what to believe is not simple, since it's complicated by a quirk of our evolutionary history. It turns out that, to start with, we all believe everything. What does that mean?

We know that we don't believe everything we hear or read. Like scientists, formulating and rejecting hypotheses, we have the ability to reject a statement as false. Not believing something, however, is more difficult than we think. Psychologists have shown that when we read a statement, we first have to believe it before we "unbelieve" it.[8] If I read "Montpellier is the capital of France," the mind must momentarily accept this as true before it determines it is false. It requires more effort to unbelieve something than believe it.

Given our evolutionary history, it makes sense why our mind's dial is set on believing first. Throughout most of our history, our senses gave us immediate and relevant information on which we were supposed to act rapidly for purposes of survival. This simple relationship between our inner and outer environments has been complicated by the evolution of language, belief, and imagination so that it became possible to believe things that don't accurately represent reality.

It's easy to be alert for falsehoods when reading or hearing things, or otherwise receiving outside information. But what about all the thoughts that we either "think up" or that "pop up" in our minds? Often, they feel immediately true because—well—they are our thoughts. Those must be true, no? Or is there one of our three minds that is more truthful than the others? It turns out that both conscious and unconscious minds can give us both right and wrong information.

The Problem Solver is great with calculating and modeling problems but gets easily tired. Also, due to its limited capacity, it doesn't deal well with lots of variables at the same time.[9] Another problem is that the Problem Solver also often does its calculations from data that the Intuiter provides. If data coming from the unconscious mind is wrong, the Problem Solver can give us wrong answers even if it does its calculations perfectly well. Let's say we are deciding whether to accept a job offer from a company. If we have an intuition that our boss will be nice and helpful (when really he is a bully), the logical conclusion to accept the offer will be a mistake.

The Intuiter, on the other hand, does most of our daily information processing and is great for lots of data, but stumbles when we are dealing with complex calculations or if we take a wrong turn with mental shortcuts.[10] The Intuiter also can't help us if we don't have enough experience (such as when we are learning a new skill). Furthermore, if our unconscious has been fed distorted data (whether through other people or media) because of structural racism or other kinds of prejudice in our environment, what feels like an instinct will be a distorted vision of others and the world. After all, the Intuiter is a data-processing machine, and if we feed it distorted data, it will give us distorted answers. Finally, when information the Intuiter holds and keeps offering to our mind as reality is outdated (such as with closed constructs), it can continually guide us in the wrong direction.

It's this last aspect of the Intuiter that is particularly relevant in our inner change work. If the unconscious mind continually surfaces frozen constructs—"I am disgusting" (Kai), "I should have helped them more" (Abhinav), "I'm not good enough" (Aisha), "Once I make enough money, I'll have the freedom to create" (Emily)—all our intuitions about ourselves and the world will be wrong. When our protagonists tried to fulfill their desires by acting on these assumptions as if they were reality, it was no wonder that they struggled to reach their wants. As we will shortly see, to move the Wheel of Self fully, we need to update the information in the unconscious.

Now that we know that the Intuiter misguides us in a way that Problem Solver can't catch, can we at least rely on the Choice-Maker to always guide us to correct decisions? Notice that the metamind doesn't process information but chooses it. It guides the flashlight of attention to one set of data or another and makes decisions. The Choice-Maker could guide us toward the truth of ourselves if it were to hold steadily our flashlight of attention on ourselves. But, as we all know from our occasional lapses into mindlessness, the process of self-examination requires lots of willpower, and when the Choice-Maker's cup of energy is emptied out, it drops the flashlight.

Where does that leave us? When working on the stalled Wheels of Self, it is crucial for the Choice-Maker to take up the flashlight of attention again and shine it on the mind itself—on frozen constructs that don't reflect reality and lead us away from our want rather than toward it. This also means illuminating some of the most unpleasant aspects of our experience (unfulfilled desires, distractors, sticky emotions, and difficult memories). Though unpleasant, this kind of self-consciousness, combined with the Problem Solver's reasoning skills, can guide us to what we need to do to reopen our old constructs, update the Intuiter, and restart our self-development. The crucial thing is to keep Choice-Maker shining that light on ourselves. Given that this takes a lot of energy, it is essential that we are well restored (which is the purpose of Technique 2) so we can do the work.

To continue your inner work, your Choice-Maker has to make a decision to direct the flashlight of attention to all different parts of your Wheel of Self and recruit the help of the Problem Solver to initiate techniques that will help transform the Intuiter.

LEARNING, OVERLEARNING, RELEARNING

How do we end up with closed constructs in our unconscious that continue to send misguiding thoughts to us? We know that constructs or beliefs are lenses through which we see the world. But what exactly are they?

Constructs or beliefs are assumptions about the world, on which we act. For example, "The floor is solid" is a construct that makes us step off the bed and on the floor in the morning without worry. Notice we don't have to think of it, or even verbalize it, we simply act as if it were true. "People who care about me will try to help me when I'm in trouble" is another construct that may help us act on the world in a predictable way. Our world is made of innumerable constructs that we build from the moment we are born onward.

How do we know whether our unconscious self has internalized inaccurate constructs about the world? We would know it by its effects. If they are correct, the world is predictable, and we usually can get to where we need to go. Even if we are not successful at getting what we want, we would understand why we have failed and what would have to change to achieve what we want. It turns out that when we act on incorrect or closed constructs in the stalled parts of our lives, we are persistently surprised, confused, and demoralized by the lack of predictability we encounter.

Aisha's beliefs about the self and the world were continually tested by her attempts and failures at getting a promotion. She was surprised that all the things she thought would work in getting her promoted (working hard, being always available, etc.), didn't work. Emily's ideas about what should make her fulfilled (her success) were continually frustrated by her dissatisfaction and restlessness. Abhinav kept being surprised by his inability to achieve one simple task (cutting down on his work) despite his repeated attempts to do so. Kai was no longer surprised by his failures to reach a healthy weight because he internalized them to the point of hopelessness. Even when he kept trying, a part of him expected failure.

Given how destructive closed and inaccurate constructs about ourselves and the world can be, we need to understand how a construct comes to be. How does it change? And why does it close or freeze?

Imagine a toddler who is building a cognitive construct of "people." At first, "people" are her caregivers, let's say a mother, father, grandparents, and aunts, and these "people" are caring and nurturing, most of the time. Then the child is taken to a daycare, where she meets other toddlers of various sizes and temperaments and other caregivers. Now she learns that "people" include both big and little people, and that sometimes these new people pay attention to her and sometimes do not. Then one day, she gets into a scuffle with another toddler over a toy, and in the heat of the moment, this previously friendly and predictable little person bites her. Now she will know that, although other kids may be friendly, sometimes they can be unpredictable and even hurt her. The construct of "people" has now expanded to include big and little people, who are sometimes friendly or unfriendly, sometimes predictable or unpredictable, and sometimes safe or dangerous. As she grows, she will slowly expand the construct of what "people" are, which should guide her through the world safely.

The construct is really a set of neural pathways activated in the brain (as all learning is). While in Chapter Six we explore the neural events that affect learning, for now let's use an easier metaphor. Imagine pouring information into the construct is like pouring liquid into a bowl (Figure 5.3). When we build a construct (that is, when we are learning), we are continually pouring more information into our constructs. In short, we are updating constructs we have about self, others, and the world so that we can better adapt to the world and act in it. Ideally, this learning and updating process never stops— the constructs stay open and information can always flow in.

So how is it then that the constructs ever "freeze" or close? Imagine that on that very day when a previously friendly kid bit her, our toddler got so distressed, that she "overlearned"—that is, experienced a neural event that put a lid on further inputs on her construct of "people." The new closed construct, "Friendly people will always eventually hurt me" stays unmodified by her subsequent experience. Once this happens, she has effectively shut down further building of the construct, no matter how relatively little information is in it. It can stay frozen in time and distort her reality for many years to come.

FIGURE 5.3 Learning, Overlearning, Relearning

She would then become distrustful and distant even from those who love her and want to be close to her. Why would this ever happen? Why would evolutionary pressures ever allow for such a departure from reality?

At this point, it would benefit us to recall that learning is mediated by our emotional system, which helps us remember what to approach and what to avoid. A sound evolutionary precaution makes it so that when we are in great danger, we learn faster how to keep ourselves safe. When the emotional system is dysregulated (that is, in distress), the nervous system gets into "high gear" and can lay down neural pathways much faster.

Let's look at an example. If we get mildly sick from eating red berries in the forest, we may avoid them until we get tempted to try them again when seeing others eating a different kind of red berries and enjoying them. This constitutes normal "open construct" learning. But if we almost die from eating red berries (and put our emotional system in distress), the construct of "Red berries equal danger" may stay seared in our brains forever. The nervous system would close the construct so that it wouldn't be able to be modified by further information. This is a "one and done" kind of learning that closes the lid on the construct. You will never touch red berries again if you value your life (no matter how much others try to convince you it is safe).

This is sound from an evolutionary perspective, since when we are in serious physical danger (let's say, accidentally step in between a mother bear and her cubs) and manage to get out alive, it would be the kind of lesson we'd never want to forget if we wanted to stay alive. We can think of it as an evolutionary overabundance of caution. However, this kind of overlearning, brought about by emotional distress, can cause serious, long-term trouble in human lives.

If we close the lid on our constructs and cannot update them despite our subsequent experience, these old, closed constructs will determine our emotions and actions in our present life. Given that they are not updated to our current reality, we are likely to try to reach our wants through misguided means and be surprised when things don't go well. The toddler who was bitten by another kid may go through the world always expecting others to hurt them, no matter how friendly and close they seem to be. Abhinav's "I'm terrible, I should have helped them more"; Aisha's "They will respect me if I work harder"; Emily's "Financial security equals freedom"; and Kai's "I'm disgusting" are all constructs that got closed early in life, and the information they needed to see themselves and the world clearly was not available to them.

Notice that occasionally, like in Kai's case, we can know that the construct is not quite right and is destructive to us, and still can't do anything about it. Kai knew that the construct "I'm disgusting" caused him a lot of distress, and he even tried to practice affirmations to replace it in his mind. But notice that instructing your conscious mind to just tell yourself that "I am good enough," or other kinds of affirmations, would be like trying to pour a liquid on top of a closed container. Unlike the body, which we can force to get out of bed at 5:00 a.m., eat kale instead of chocolate, and run around the block when it would prefer to sit on the couch, we can't force the mind to do anything. We can give the Problem Solver instructions about what to think, but if the instructions are different than what the Intuiter thinks, the Problem Solver will be easily overwhelmed by the multitude of messages from the unconscious mind that will pop up in the window of awareness. This helps explain why so-called positive thinking is so tiring and often ineffective.

We all know that having negative constructs about the self can lead to a multitude of negative life outcomes. But asking people to change their negative self-constructs just by positive thinking (either through repetitive mantras or reasoned positive statements) ignores the mechanism of how our minds work. Any change in how we think daily will have to include changes both in the conscious and the unconscious mind. And because the conscious mind doesn't control the unconscious (like telling ourselves what we want to dream about tonight), *what is necessary is that we use the conscious mind to structure experiences that restructure the unconscious mind.* This is what the techniques in this book are aiming for.

The Problem Solver is crucial in solving the issue of frozen constructs, but not by ordering the rest of the mind about. Instead, with the Choice-Maker's help, it will gather the information necessary to design experiences that will allow the rebuilding of frozen constructs that distort our view of ourselves and the world.

How does that happen? It turns out that there is a third process, in addition to learning and overlearning. It is **relearning**, where we have experiences that take the lid off the construct and allow information to flow in again. In Chapter Six, we will address different kinds of relearning, but first we need to know how to recognize closed constructs in our lives.

FINDING CLOSED CONSTRUCTS

Before we start exploring closed constructs, a word of caution. The exploration from this point onward in the book could lead you to reflect on difficult moments in your life and bring up painful memories and emotions. Many of you may prefer to do this kind of exploration with the support of a therapist, psychologist, counselor, coach, or friend. No matter what way you decide to explore the rest of this book (with support or by yourself), it will be the right way for you.

Let's now turn to the problem of closed constructs. Scientists studying belief change have long been aware that some constructs are updated normally while others appear to be "immune" to change.[11] Given that we generate thousands of constructs about ourselves, others, and the world, how would we be able to detect the ones that are closed?

In the previous section, we said that accurate constructs "work"— when we see the world through their lens, the world behaves in predictable ways, and we know what to do to get what we want. Let's say that we act on the open construct that we don't swim very well. It would be predictable to us that we are all right in a pool and more hesitant to enter the sea. We'd also know that if we wanted to swim in the sea when it's windy, we'd need more swimming lessons.

On the other hand, when the construct is closed, it keeps us from getting to where we want to go, and we don't know why. If we have a construct "I have excellent interviewing skills" but then keep failing to get a job because the construct is inaccurate, we are likely to keep being surprised by it. If the construct is implicit (not verbalized as a belief), it would be very difficult to draw a connection between it and a poor outcome. This is why it's important to put the construct in words, as you were asked to do in the last step of Technique 3.

Once you have some of your constructs written down, it's time to explore which of them are closed. What are the markers of thoughts that betray closed constructs?

1. We had them many times before (in identical form). A construct that is forged in the emotional heat of a dangerous situation is impermeable to new information. It means that it does not change, adapt, or evolve. Did we have the same thought many times before, in identical form? If yes, it could be a clue there is a closed construct generating the thoughts. Then, it would be worthwhile asking ourselves, When was the first time we had this thought? When Kai reflected on the thought "I am disgusting," he realized this thought has been with him since his early childhood (probably first grade onward), and usually when his father was around. When Emily asked herself where her thought "You need financial success to have freedom to create" came from, she could point to the conversation with her father in her last year of high school, when she asked him about going to art school.

Even if we don't remember exactly the moment we had the thought, it's enough to reflect broadly about what stage in our life we started having this thought. Let's say we've had thoughts like "I'm lonely, no one is there for me" for as long as we can remember. We can start by asking ourselves, Have I felt this as a toddler? as a pre-schooler? in elementary school? in high school? and so on. Even if we get a broad sense of the time when the construct started, it will be helpful as we work on them.

2. They generalize across situations, people, and time. Thoughts that are impermeable constructs tend to be broad or categorical generalizations. Words like "always," "never," and "should" are frequently part of the belief statement. A person who turns off their alarm one morning, and thinks, "I'm no good, I'm lazy" is generalizing from one situation to their whole self. A child whose parents have divorced can think either, "Sometimes love doesn't last" or "Love never lasts." Someone betrayed by a friend may say, "Joe betrayed me" or "People are not to be trusted." We need to catch broad, rigid generalizations about the self, others, and the world. When Abhinav thought of his parents' suffering and believed, "This is not what they sacrificed for," and "I should have helped them more," he was generalizing across time. His parents used to suffer but were now comfortable. Abhinav didn't help much as a kid but has helped his parents enormously since then. None of these changes registered in Abhinav's constructs. They stayed closed.

3. We are afraid of new information. When we have a closed construct, and the lid is on, receiving information that is contradictory to what we believe is distressing. Because we can't input the information into our own closed construct (by simply thinking it), the experience gives us a sense of dissonance or inner rupture. This is why we often go out of our way to avoid disconfirming information.[12] It's difficult to know something and internally feel the opposite. For example, knowing we are competent (by looking at the objective evidence of our successes) but feeling inside as if we are not gives us a classic experience of imposter syndrome.

The difficulty of holding these opposing inner and outer realities is also why we may be habitually drawn to media sources that we trust not to tell us something that could challenge our constructs. By only interacting with predictable sources of media, we don't have to be continually on guard. In the same way, we may systematically disbelieve *everything* the "other media" says, so we don't have to keep parsing what to believe and what to discard.

When Aisha had to receive her biannual performance review, she used to dread it. The reason was that on one (conscious) level, she knew she had both the technical and leadership skills to be promoted, and yet feared she wouldn't be. Not being promoted conflicted with her "The world should be just" construct. Notice that the aspirational "should" really acted as a defense against reality— which is that the world wasn't always just. Aisha also avoided talking about work to friends who have left her company due to perceived racism in the management. If Aisha acted on the world knowing that it wasn't always just, she wouldn't keep trying to do what would get her a promotion in a world that *is* just. Instead, she would look for new solutions. Not being promoted also reinforced other closed constructs that used to show up in Aisha's mind when she was stressed, such as "I'm not smart enough" or "I'm not ready for leadership." The history and frequency with which these categorical statements recurred were a further indication to Aisha that many of her constructs about herself and the world were closed.

TECHNIQUE 4: RESEARCHING CONSTRUCTS

We now move to the technique that will help us research our constructs. We will start where we left off in Technique 3—with a list of constructs we've come up with by exploring our persistent negative emotions. In Figure 5.4 are step-by-step instructions with an illustrative example.

STEP 1: *Take the list of constructs/beliefs from box 4 in Technique 3 (Figure 4.7) and transfer them to the first box in Figure 5.4. Then ask yourselves the following questions: Have you had this thought many times before, in a similar form? Does it include a generalization (across time, people, or situations)? Does it include the words always, never, must, or should? These questions will help you get a sense of whether the construct you are researching has been overgeneralized, indicating that it hasn't been updated with more detailed and precise information over time.*

Example: Imagine our adult life is plagued with feelings of loneliness, which persists despite having a loving family and friends who

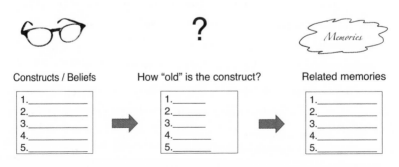

FIGURE 5.4 Technique 4: Researching Constructs/Beliefs

care about us. Even during family gatherings, we feel empty, like we are separated from all the others by an invisible barrier. While exploring what thoughts precede this feeling, we discover these constructs: "No one is ever there for me. I'll never feel the connection others feel." We realize this same thought has been showing up in our mind in this, or a very similar form, for years. In this first step, we find that the thoughts include those general terms—"ever," "always"—which points us to the possibility this is a closed construct.

STEP 2: *What is the earliest time you had this thought? You don't need to pinpoint the exact instance, just broadly your stage of life. This question will take you back to how the belief originated in the first place, historically. You may think, "I always had this thought," or "This is just how I am," but in that case, you can remind yourself that you are not born with constructs—that they are constructed (built) through interactions with our environment (other people). One way to find the origin period is to think of yourself as a toddler, as a preschooler, then during elementary school, and so on, while asking yourself, Did I have these thoughts then? Once you have an idea of the time period, place it in the middle box of Figure 5.4.*

Example: Trying to locate how early the thoughts of loneliness originated, we can start reviewing by asking ourselves, Did I feel this as a toddler? We may not remember. Did we have these thoughts as preschoolers? No, we played with our friends and were actually feeling rather joyous. Now that we think of it, preschool was really a blissful time, the last time that we felt truly connected to others around us. How about elementary school? This gives us pause— elementary school was very alienating. Yes, elementary school is maybe the earliest we had thoughts like "There is no one there for me, I'll never feel connected."

STEP 3: *Do you have any memories that are related to this construct? Often memories related to closed constructs can stay very active in our* *unconscious mind. The reason is that the lid most often comes down when we are emotionally dysregulated (distressed), which tends to make memories of those events particularly vivid. You can write down as many memories for each construct as come to your mind. If you don't have any related memories of a closed construct, that is perfectly fine; you can simply write down the construct and around when you think the lid had closed on it.*

Example: One of the memories that may come up as we reflect on our construct of being lonely is coming back from school, into the empty house, and being by ourselves until our parents came back from work a few hours later. After some reflection, we realize that it must have been in the fourth grade. Before that, our grandmother would have picked us up from school and then made us a snack at home, and we would have chatted and played until Mom and Dad came home. In the fourth grade, our grandmother passed away. We can write down any memories that come up in relation to the constructs we are examining in the last box of Figure 5.4.

Once you have found which of your constructs are still closed, around what age the lid came down on the construct, and perhaps even a few memories of how it happened, it is time to move the last part of the Wheel of Self—your embodied past.

CHAPTER SIX

(EM)BODIED PAST

We have arrived at the final stage of our work on the Wheel of Self. You have learned how to rediscover your core wants, restore yourself, and find sticky emotions and the closed constructs that caused them. Finally, in Technique 4, you were asked to probe for memories that could help you understand when and how your constructs may have closed. There is one more technique left to learn. Given that closed constructs are neural pathways carried in our body, just knowing what they are, and even how they came to be, doesn't make them reopen automatically. Abhinav, Kai, Emily, and Aisha all managed to uncover early experiences that created closed constructs and halted their development in some part of the self. Yet, just knowing that didn't produce the transformation, didn't restart the Wheel of Self. As we saw in Chapter Five, the Problem Solver can't *force* the Intuiter to update or change the construct.

Insight may be necessary, but is not sufficient, for transformation. It needs to be joined with an experience that opens the lid to the closed construct, and only then can we update it, getting the Wheel of Self to move again. The difficulty is that the source experience that closed the construct is most often *in the past*. To update it (relearn) we need to go to that source experience, to the past, to lay down a new set of neural pathways. How is that even possible? To understand what makes relearning possible, we need to explore the part of ourselves that allows us to have a past in the first place—our **body**.

WHAT IS A BODY FOR?

To say the word "body" is to bring up a set of associations: height, weight, skin elasticity, cholesterol, blood pressure, and heart rate. We think of measurements of various kinds, how we feel when we look in the mirror, or what happens when some part of the body refuses to comply with the daily demands life puts upon it. The central associations we have with our bodies are likely connected to their appearance, physiological (dys)function, and maybe even their inevitable demise. All of this, however, doesn't tell us what bodies are for.

From an evolutionary perspective, we can think of our *bodies as vessels made of the past meant to act in the present while looking to the future.* The first obvious thing that bodies do is move around to meet their wants. Unlike trees in a forest that wait for the rain to fall, we can amble about, find a water source, and drink. Unlike plant life, which has limited mobility, our bodies allow us to actively reach our various wants.

The second function of the body is to carry our past. We often forget that all our learnings, all our skills, and even many of our short and long-term goals are nothing more than projected fragments of our past experiences. They are carried by our brain and nervous system, as well as the muscles, joints, organs, blood cells, immune cells, and many other constituents of the body whose actions in the present moment are altered by the "memory" of the past. We make our future by combining past experiences and learnings with current motivations and potentials. Bodies hold our learnings and employ them forward as we encounter new situations. They are magnificent and subtle learning machines.

Why use the term "body" to describe the container that carries forward our learnings, rather than more specific terms such as "brain" or "nervous system," which evoke parts of our bodies that have evolved for this particular purpose? For one, all parts of the body have the capacity to learn from their experience and carry on "memories" to adapt to novel environments. Think of the muscles and joints of virtuoso musicians or athletes, organs of transplant patients, or immune cells strengthened by an encounter with a virus. But a much more important reason to use the term "body" is to encourage a movement away from seeing it in terms of measurements and recognize it instead as a vessel that carries our learnings to help us in novel situations. Only once we understand the role bodies have in reenacting the past, including past overlearned constructs, can we use our conscious mind to apply levers that will guide us to different future experiences.

If the body carries our learnings, it also carries our overlearned constructs that distort our experience. From the last chapter, we know that overlearning happens in dangerous situations where the emotional system tries to protect us by making our defenses reflexive and invariable. We may reflexively shun closeness to others to avoid getting hurt, or reflexively overwork in the hope of feeling worthy. The closed constructs that feed these unconscious patterns are carried *in the body*, so it will be *in the body* that changes required for relearning will have to occur. But before we find out how to intervene to re-open our closed constructs, we will explore a group uniquely vulnerable to overlearning.

Children's Vulnerability to Overlearning

Although constructs can close at any stage of our lives, why is it that many of them close during childhood? We know that constructs start closing in situations of high danger and emotional stress. Children's vulnerability to overlearning has to do with a large period of almost complete dependence on caregivers they experience while growing up. Thankfully, we know that children are particularly adapted to learning, not just in how to navigate the physical but the social world as well. We call children "little sponges" because they absorb everything from their environment, not only things that their parents want them to learn. On the one hand, they are learning to walk, to feed themselves, to talk; but while doing so, they are also learning how to experience and relate to themselves and the people who surround them.

Given how dependent children are on caregiving by adults around them, it is natural they are very sensitive to changes in the emotional tone of adults, particularly anything that indicates distress and displeasure with them. Children are highly attuned to caregivers' facial expressions, tones of voice, gestures, and movements.[1] Adults may get socially rejected and abandoned, but if they can take care of their basic functions, rejection will not likely result in death. For very young children, social abandonment equals death. Being appreciated, cared for, and loved is, for them, a matter of life and death. As a consequence, children's emotional systems are likely to treat all interactions with others as emotionally charged. What does this mean in terms of the development of constructs?

Even in the best of circumstances, childhood can be stressful. Our cognitive maps are not yet properly filled out, we are not yet skilled at processing our emotions, and we are still building our willpower. Add to that our ultimate dependence and the danger it implies, and it follows that childhood would be the time we would be most vulnerable to many of our constructs closing prematurely. As adults, we can place any particularly stressful event (say, losing a job) against everything we know about our skills, education, and the job market. We can deploy our social skills to ask for help, get more education, and find opportunities to get another job. A young child who has been mocked in school by their peers, on the other hand, often has neither the language skills nor emotional and cognitive abilities to deal with the situation or reach out to others for help. We will not be surprised to find that many of our constructs may have closed long before our adult troubles began.

Significant Life Events

Now that we have examined why we overlearn and are particularly vulnerable to it in childhood, it's time to consider how the construct's lid closes. In the previous chapter, we discussed overlearning as a one-off scenario, as if the lid simply locked on the construct in situations of extreme danger. However, there are degrees of how closed the construct becomes. We can think of the lid as not simply on or off but in various states of tightness, requiring different degrees of effort to reopen the construct to new information. What determines the tightness of the construct's lid is how much emotional distress (and potential danger) the person experiences while learning about themselves or the world.

The relationship between stress and learning tends to follow an inverted U-shaped curve.[2] Imagine you are studying for an exam. The more stress you have, the faster you'd learn—up to a point. This is when the stress gets so high that the learning suffers. We can think of that high point of stress as a time at which a lid is introduced to our constructs. From that point on, the more stress we have is like the lid tightening further and further on the relevant construct, and the less we are able to learn.[3] What we end up with is a continuum.[4] On the one end, we have fully open constructs that we can continue updating, on the other end, completely closed ones, and in between we find constructs with various degrees of openness.

When children are exposed to an extremely stressful situation, it can produce trauma, which often fully closes some of their constructs. These events (called "adverse childhood events," or ACEs) include physical, emotional, or sexual abuse, physical and emotional neglect, parental addictions, mental illness, violence, or incarceration.[5] Those who have suffered through ACEs will often seek out the support of psychotherapists, psychologists, counselors, or psychiatrists, as they work through their traumas. The study of ACEs continues a long tradition of the study of what life events negatively impact mental health outcomes.[6] What we'll focus on here, however, is the "in-between" area, which lies *between fully open and closed constructs.*

What is this middle ground? It's situations that are not as extreme as ones contributing to trauma but still cause a tightening of the lid on the constructs. We can call these **significant events**, because while they don't have the same visibility as adverse events, they still negatively impact our constructs and, therefore, our life outcomes. What usually makes these events invisible is that they don't seem extreme, or even noteworthy, while at the same time they have a powerful effect on our self-development.

Being teased as a child or embarrassed by a schoolmate, receiving a cutting remark by a teacher or a parent, or simply witnessing what we perceive as a disapproving expression on their faces in an important moment—all could cause overlearning. In short, any vivid situation in which we are distressed (dysregulated) emotionally and feel rejected, unloved, ashamed, or marginalized, no matter what the intentions of those around us, can cause the "wounds" that lay down neural pathways that can be activated by stressful situations for years to come. Even the absence of information—being left ignorant about finances, sex, or spirituality—can leave lasting emotional marks that continue to slow or stall our development. Notice that growing up even within most loving, best-intentioned families doesn't prevent children from experiencing these significant events, either inside or outside the home. Let us look at Aisha's, Kai's, Abhinav's, and Emily's constructs again and explore their significant events.

When Aisha completed Technique 4, she noticed that the two constructs that would activate under stress were "I am not good enough" and "They know my potential better than I do." Note that Aisha was cognitively aware of her superior skills, yet the stressful work situations would activate "I am not good enough" nonetheless. When thinking about how early these beliefs started, she had two memories that stood out. The first was from elementary school. She was good at math, and her hand would go up whenever the teacher would put a "hard problem" on the blackboard. But the teacher would keep calling on white kids. He would only call on her if no one else knew the answer, and even then, he looked displeased. When she complained to the teacher that he never called on her, he said he was simply giving everyone a chance to learn. Young Aisha's distress from being discriminated against was met with "the world is just" information—closing the construct about the potential injustice in the world. She internalized the lesson that she can't trust her intuition about how others treat her. Maybe the teacher is very fair and she is selfish, taking up all the space. She stopped raising her hand in class.

The second memory was from years later and again had to do with a teacher, this time in high school. Aisha's calculus teacher, who she felt saw her talent and encouraged her academically, asked her one day to stay after class and speak to her about her future. The teacher said, "You should really consider community college. It will be a much better fit for you than university." Aisha, who had by this point already applied to several universities, left class that day feeling disoriented, disappointed, and pained. She was accepted and went to university anyway, but the conflict between believing that people can seem to care about her and, at the same time, diminish her potential reinforced the construct "They know my potential better than I do." Believing this allowed her to keep thinking of her teachers as caring adults not affected by the structural racism that permeated her environment.

What about Kai? Despite the continual issue his father had made of his weight in his childhood (taking him for runs at 6:00 a.m. and removing food from his plate on a regular basis), it was a different memory that emerged when he reflected on the construct "I am disgusting." Kai's mother had encouraged him to start dressing, choosing his clothes and putting them on himself during preschool. By the time he started the first grade, at age six, he could choose his outfit and fully dress and was rather proud of that achievement. One morning during first grade, Kai's father, who usually left for work before the rest of the family awoke, stayed home since he was unwell. Kai was very proud to show his dad that he could dress himself. He got a bit delayed, though, and when his father entered his room to get him to come down for breakfast, Kai was still in his underwear, choosing his clothes. At that moment, as his father looked at him, Kai recognized a clear expression of disgust on his father's face. It only lasted a moment, and his father left the room to leave him to dress, but the expression and internalized construct "I am disgusting," had stayed with Kai ever since.

For Abhinav, as with Kai, it was an accidental moment he witnessed that returned to him when he explored the construct "They sacrificed and overworked for me; it's my turn to sacrifice and overwork for them." Once, when he was ten, he was awakened by the sounds of his father coming back from his night shift at the factory around 6:00 a.m. As usual, his mother was already up, waiting for his father and getting ready for work. Abhinav snuck downstairs and overheard them whispering in the kitchen. His father's arm was crudely bandaged. He worked in construction, and Abhinav heard him say he couldn't work for another two weeks. They were planning how to stretch the money they had left to feed the family for the rest of the month. He couldn't catch all they were saying, but they looked worried and exhausted. He went back upstairs without being seen or heard. The next morning, as on all other mornings, his mother made him and his brother breakfast and sent them to school with a snack. Abhinav felt as if he had dreamt the scene that he witnessed, yet he knew it was true and that his parents hid all their concerns and stresses from him and his brother, so as not to worry them. That moment would often return to him, bringing guilt and impetus to work even harder, to somehow make his parents' sacrifices "worth it."

Finally, Emily thought that what caused her construct "Only financial security can lead to freedom to create" was her conversation with her father about art school. But while exploring her memories, she encountered another, earlier one that still stung her with discomfort and even shame. She was about eight years old when her parents threw a ten-year wedding anniversary party at their home. It was summer, and people were milling around the pool and the garden. Her parents hired a string quartet, and musicians were playing on a small, elevated stage in one part of the garden. Emily loved watching them—they seemed sophisticated and played beautifully. She thought they were on the elevated stage because they were guests of honor. But when it was time for a break, and they left their instruments on the chairs to step down to take a bite to eat with other guests, she watched her mother quickly approach them. She was talking in low tones and gesturing toward the kitchen. It took only a few seconds, but Emily understood that they were being sent to the kitchen to eat with the servers. To her parents they were not guests of honor, they were "hired help"—the same as their cook and cleaners. She felt stung with shame as if she were the one who was humiliated. It was this moment that started the process that ended with her acquiescing to her father's wishes that she not go to the art school.

This is how **significant events** happen—they can be short, accidental, passing episodes that still leave us shaken, pained, and with constructs about ourselves and others that have started to close. Even if these beliefs are not active all the time, they show up when some aspects of the situation we encounter activate our old neural pathways. And although not extreme, these early situations can tighten the lid on our constructs in a way that makes it difficult to update and modify our beliefs about ourselves and the world. It is these beliefs that we need to reopen to experience if we want to restart the stalled areas of our development.

INGREDIENTS FOR TRANSFORMATIONAL CHANGE

What does it take to **relearn**—to loosen the lid on our impermeable constructs, to reopen our beliefs to experience? What are the essential conditions under which relearning happens?

To answer that question, we need to cast our net widely. Most of the everyday change that we witness happens gradually. Seasons change, children grow, and we age gradually. New languages are learned gradually, as are our habitual routines. Expertise, friendship, and relationships are all built slowly, over time. "Gradually" is the term we use for linear transformation over time. It is how open constructs adapt and change with the input of new experiences, which is almost continual. We can think of it as slow change. But to understand how to loosen the lid of the closed construct, we need to examine a different, nonlinear model of change.

Rapid Relearning

What do we mean by "nonlinear" here? It means that change doesn't build gradually but happens rapidly, like an earthquake. We've all known individuals who "turn over the new leaf" in their lives seemingly overnight. How is that possible? It turns out that when we are in danger and our emotional system is in distress (dysregulated), the nervous system gets into "high gear" and can build new neural pathways more quickly. Instead of slow, gradual change, we'd see dramatic and sudden transformations. While we could be trying to quit smoking for years (gradually), having our physician show us an X-ray of our lungs (and possible lung cancer), could cause us to quit smoking overnight. This is why in many countries cigarette packages have graphic visual warnings—the idea is to cause enough emotional dysregulation to produce a rapid change.

Studies show that emotional dysregulation happens both before experiencing trauma[7] and post-traumatic growth.[8] This means that the dysregulation can either produce closing of the construct or re-opening of it.[9] Whether the change is positive or negative depends not only on the intensity of the emotional distress but also whether or not it is caused by external circumstances (others or the world) or is a part of our own exploration of change (self-induced). For example, being pushed out of a plane with a parachute attached to us would have a very different effect than going skydiving. One is forced, the other a voluntary dysregulation.

We also see emotional dysregulation before a "quantum change" when individuals with a long history of drinking suddenly recover, as well as just before their relapse.[10] Even in therapy, the "breakthrough" sessions are preceded by a spike in emotional arousal.[11] Notice that emotional dysregulation is like a force that can be used either to shut the lid down on constructs or open them back up, depending on the intensity and voluntariness of the event. What we see then is that

emotional dysregulation provides the first ingredient that is essential to a transformative change.[12]

The second ingredient is the "content" or information that will be "poured into" the new construct.[13] Think of it as a **new framework** (a way of looking at ourselves and the world). The nervous system has activated to lay down new pathways quickly, but what exactly it will encode depends on what information it gets. In the earlier example, a person confronted with an X-ray of potential lung cancer may think "I'm so glad I saw this in time" and stop smoking, or think "I don't believe this doctor" and smoke even more. What they are encoding into the construct is new information, a new framework of what smoking means to them.

Notice that if we get emotionally dysregulated but have no new framework through which to see the world, our nervous system will simply go back to its previous state and the construct will remain unchanged. Think of watching a horror movie. You get emotionally dysregulated then go back to normal. If there is no new framework, the dysregulation doesn't result in change, simply activation and deactivation of the neural pathways.

What we see, then, are two conditions for any technique that claims to attempt rapid **relearning,** whether positive or negative:

1. **Emotional dysregulation** (which loosens the lid of the closed construct by making the neural system ready for rapid change); and
2. **A new framework/experience** that will be poured into the reopened construct.

Now that we understand what conditions are required for a rapid change in the self, we need to distinguish between a developmental relearning experience and a negative or coercive one.

They Break Us to Remake Us

The fact that emotional dysregulation precedes rapid self-change has been an open secret, culturally, for millennia. Any social group that wanted to control individuals' behavior has built techniques to reproduce the dysregulation of the emotional system prior to imposing their own constructs and so inducing the new set of behaviors.

Ancient rites of passage are seen by anthropologists as technologies of transformation, the making of a new person. What many of the rites had in common is that those who underwent them were exposed to both physiological and psychological stressors. For example, in a hunting tribe, a young boy could be violently and ceremoniously removed from his mother and the home, expelled into the forest where his tasks would be to survive for days without food or water and hunt a dangerous animal. In addition to days without food, sleep, and exposure to physical danger, rites could often include painful tattooing or piercings—an alarming situation for the emotional system. After the boy was fully emotionally dysregulated, there would be a ceremony of the return to the community where the elders would give the inductee a new construct, a new role, and a new personhood. Note that if the tribe had to wait until boys decided they wanted to become hunters, they would have waited a long time, particularly since the boys could choose to do other things than hunt and kill large game. Instead, the tribe "made" hunters out of boys. The rites would start with separation and end with reaggregation back into the community.[14]

We can see a similar process in attempts at thought reform or brainwashing of prisoners of war. They are subjected to sleeplessness (noise, lights), being chained in painful stress positions, humiliation, isolation, or crowding—all deeply dysregulating. These are followed by interviews in which the interrogator gives the prisoner a new construct ("Let me help you. This is how you can think of it.") in exchange for prisoners changing their beliefs or alliances.[15]

Hazing, an abuse of prospective group members, is often marked by sleep deprivation and physical and sexual humiliation, combined with the newcomer having to pledge themselves to the group's values.[16] Cults often demand breaks with family, friends, and all other sources of emotional support, which are deeply dysregulating, and replace these relationships with a rigid set of values and rules that the cult inductee has to follow—the new framework for life.

We are likely to encounter similar strategies in our professional and personal lives. Some corporations warn their young applicants that if they get the job, they will have little sleep, high stress, no personal time, and will have to attend mandatory social activities where the organization's "values" are imprinted and enacted. Many personal transformational and leadership training groups include public sharing of difficult personal challenges (without the opportunity to "pass" and not share) as a way to "bond" the group and have them align with group norms.

What all these situations have in common is an external application of physiological and psychological pressure on an individual, to be followed by a new framework that is beneficial for the institution, group, or the individual in charge of this process. Knowing about coercive change can act as an inoculation against attempts at it. If we are being dysregulated (whether by lack of sleep or food, or by being forced to do or share uncomfortable things, particularly in public), we are being made pliable to other-induced change. If we can notice it, we can stop the process.

Whereas in the last section, we saw that relearning requires both emotional dysregulation and a new construct (taking a lid off the old construct and pouring new information into it), here we specify conditions for coercive change that shapes the person toward the goals of the coercive agent:

1. The dysregulation is externally induced by the coercive agent;
2. The new construct is designed and presented by actors who want to control our values, thoughts, emotions, and behavior.

Why is this so problematic? First, when others induce emotional dysregulation in our self-system, we cannot gauge it or control its intensity in the same way we could if we were guiding the process. Second, our self-development cannot proceed naturally if the new framework (a new way of seeing ourselves or the world) is imposed by others. Often, if a group is trying to control our behavior, they don't have an interest in us keeping our constructs open; we are more predictable if the constructs are closed shut with the framework of their choosing. They are changing us, not in the direction of our potential but into what they want us to be. Like trauma, this kind of change is not self-developmental in nature.

If we are interested in transformational change in some part of our life that has been resistant to change, *we need to be in charge of the process.* We need a technique through which we can induce **voluntary emotional dysregulation** and pour into the newly reopened construct a **new framework** that is **of our own choosing**, and not imposed.

RELEARNING TO HEAL

What would a healthy relearning look like? What are the essential ingredients of relearning that are self-guided, self-developmental, and lead to opening rather than further closing of our constructs?

We already have the two basic components of developmental transformation: **voluntary emotional dysregulation** (opening the lid) and **self-generated new framework** (new information or an experience that is poured into the construct). Now we need to examine how to employ these conditions to help make the self-change process developmental rather than coercive or traumatizing.

One great source of understanding the conditions for healing and opening closed constructs in a healthy way comes from work on trauma that has been actively done by the psychological community over the last century. Trauma expert Bessel van der Kolk outlined many different healing techniques in his book *The Body Keeps the Score*. Some of them include "bottom-up" approaches that help trauma victims feel reconnected and safe in their own bodies.[17] Others are "top-down" techniques where we use our powers of language, imagination, and insight to unfreeze the old constructs. To help us design a technique, we will look at different characteristics of the various "top-down" approaches.

The first pattern that can be noticed in van der Kolk's description of "top-down" techniques is that many of them include people reexperiencing the original traumatic events either by writing about it[18], talking about it, or even physically enacting it within the safe confines of a therapeutic session.[19] Mentally and emotionally reliving the significant event both provides the emotional dysregulation necessary for making the nervous system plastic and also activates the original closed construct (set of neural pathways) that is to be reopened and updated by a new framework or experience. By doing this, we activate and reexperience the part of ourselves that froze at the age when it was closed: our "inner child."

When Kai would think of (or replay in his mind) the moment when his father showed disgust at Kai's body, he would get naturally dysregulated. The same was the case when Aisha was thinking of her

teachers, Abhinav of his parents, and Emily of her parents' interaction with musicians at their party. By mentally and emotionally
reliving the event, they would be dysregulated and emotionally
transported to the younger versions of themselves, whose emotional
responses seemed stuck in time. The *dysregulation inherent in mentally and emotionally reliving the significant event reopens the lid of our
closed constructs.*

The second pattern that can be noticed in van der Kolk's description of the "top-down" techniques has to do with what kind of new
frameworks or experiences would pour into the reopened construct.
We already know that it won't be developmentally useful if the framework is one that someone else imposes or coerces us into. Instead,
*the new framework is what we would have needed at the time of the
significant event (whether support, affection, protection, information, or
intervention) to have fully processed it then.*

What is it that Kai or Aisha needed, despite the complexity of
their significant events, for their constructs not to close? Kai needed
another adult to tell him that he is beautiful and loved and that even
his father can get things wrong. Aisha needed guidance to help her
accept that even the people who think they are well-intentioned can
suffer from prejudice and mislead us; that the world is not as just as
we hope for, but that we can work toward it. The new framework is
like solving the problem of a significant event backward in time.
What were additional experiences and information that were needed?
Then we build new neural pathways that incorporate that information, on top of the old ones, activated by the reexperiencing of the
event. It doesn't erase the event; it fills it with additional experience
and updates our newly reopened constructs.

The patterns that can be observed in van der Kolk's work help
fill the picture of how to design our last technique. It needs to include the following:

1. **Voluntary emotional dysregulation** *(that can be produced by mental and emotional reliving of the significant event)*; and
2. **Self-generated new framework/experience** *(that includes what was missing at the time to allow full processing of the event)*.

Once Kai would be able to relive, mentally and emotionally, the event with his father (dysregulation) but manage to incorporate the affection, presence, and support he needed at the time (new framework), this intervention would allow him a targeted and rapid reshaping of the very neural pathways that were "frozen in time." In doing so, he would have updated his constructs, restructured his neural pathways, retrained his unconscious, and reprocessed his old emotions.

Now let's turn to the components you would need to have ready to design a relearning experience to update your closed constructs: (1) Finding the significant events that caused the closing of the constructs, and (2) finding a new framework or experience that would have allowed the processing of the significant event.

Part 1: Finding Significant Events

Before you start exploring which memories of significant events you could work on when updating your constructs, another word of caution. This book is intended to help you explore and reprocess significant events that have caused some of your self-development wheels to stall. It presupposes that you feel safe enough to do the exploration on your own, given your history. If that is not the case, and you don't feel safe, it's important you find the support you need, whether with your family, friends, or therapeutic professionals. This book is to be used the way that works best for you—by yourself or with the support of others. The important thing is to find your own way.

In Technique 4, you listed memories associated with each of the closed constructs. How would you know which of these you should work on? To answer that question, you need to know a few things about memories.

Memories are not video recordings of our past as much as summaries of emotionally important situations and their outcomes, embedded in our emotional system to help us navigate our present reality.[20] The "regular" memories come with a "time stamp"—they are processed in a way that allows us to know them as memories every time we recall them. They are narrative so that we can use language to describe them, and we can place them within the context of our life. Most importantly, they are not likely to show up uninvited in our minds. *We go to the memory, rather than the memory coming to us.*

Memories of significant and adverse events have very different qualities. They are often experienced not in the mind but in our bodies—as fragments of sights, smells, sounds, and movements that we can still reexperience in our body when the memory shows up.[21] Whenever Kai would think of the moment he saw his father's disgusted expression, he would feel a shudder and a chill in his body, just as he did when he saw it for the first time. More importantly, these memories can be intrusive. They can be triggered both during the day, evoked by smells, sounds, touch, or images, and during the night, generating nightmares. They can also be triggered by our thoughts, turning our minds back to our past and leaving us vulnerable to forget where we are, what we are doing, and with whom. Why would our unconscious mind keep reactivating these old experiences? If we remember from the past chapters, an unresolved problem in the unconscious is always in the "now." Therefore, bringing it to our attention is the way for the Intuiter to signal that we have some more reprocessing to do.[22]

What does this mean for how to select memories for Technique 5? You can ask yourself two questions:

1. **Which memories from your past intrude on your mind when you think of the construct?** These are the memories that pop up unannounced, that simply show up when we are distressed, and are sometimes accompanied by sensory fragments (flashbacks of sights, sounds, smells, or visceral sensations of discomfort).

2. **Do you still have strong emotions about these events from the past?** It's easy to assume that it's natural to always feel strong negative emotions about significant events from the past. From the chapter on emotions, we know that emotions are meant to be temporary, to come and go. So if they are staying, it means that our past threats, losses, or obstacles need to be reprocessed.

If the answer to both questions is yes, then you have good candidates you can work on in the next technique. But before we do that, we need to understand how to find a new framework or experience that we can pour into the new construct once the construct lid is open.

Part 2: Finding New Frameworks

We can think of new frameworks for the problems we encountered during significant events in two ways: as information and as experiences.

If we think of a new framework as information, we will follow the beginning steps of cognitive behavioral therapy—we will notice the unhelpful, frozen cognitive constructs and explore what other more helpful ones would include.

For example, when Aisha is reflecting on the closed construct "Maybe they are right, and I am not good enough" while thinking of her teacher who encouraged her to attend community college rather than university, we can think of what kind of realistic constructs she needed to hear at 17 that would have prevented the "I'm not good enough" construct from closing. This would probably include an insight that even people who care for us can be impacted by prejudice; that people we admire can sometimes disappoint us; that a few negative experiences don't mean that we can't find teachers and mentors with whom we feel safe and supported. It may also include reflections on how hard it is to be disappointed and not seen by people we admire, but that, again, is something that we can handle and we can continue in life trusting our instincts about our skills and capabilities.

One benefit of working on old constructs is that as we age and gain more experience and insight, we may already have the information we need to update them. A good question to ask at this point is how can we "have" this new information and still have a closed construct on the same topic? This also raises the question of why cognitive insight by itself doesn't always lead to transformation. From what we know about relearning, it seems that just having cognitive insights (without the accompanying dysregulation) doesn't rewrite our original constructs but, rather, sits separately as an informational fragment, not part of our unconscious instincts. The Problem Solver can have the new information but can't force the Intuiter to update its memory stores with it. It appears that for the transformation, we need the *dual activation* of the emotional and mind systems. *Emotion dysregulation makes the nervous system more "plastic," and then we apply insights on the same constructs that were closed.*

Another way to think about the new framework is not as information but as experience. If we think of Kai's case where, at age six, he was trying to process the expression of disgust on his father's face, the new information—that his body isn't disgusting, that he was still lovable for who he is—is not likely to be easily communicable to the "six-year-old self." One easy exercise to find new frames is to imagine our younger sibling, a child, a niece, or a nephew, in a similar situation. What would we have done if we walked into the room? In the case of Kai, we would have likely told little Kai that his body was not disgusting but beautiful and also comforted him so that he felt loved, safe, appreciated, and protected. For constructs that have closed in earlier parts of our lives, what we are "rewriting" in our neural system is not just information but the experience (of being safe, seen, loved, and protected). As adults, we can now offer what we have needed to our younger selves.

Note that this ability, to use the experience in a top-down way for transformative purposes, will only work if we have, at some point in our lives, felt safe, loved, and protected. In cases of extreme trauma, where patients may have gone a lifetime without these experiences, building them takes more "bottom-up" techniques and longer therapeutic interventions. If, as you look for new frames, you feel that you are not sure what the new framework is or what the experience is supposed to feel like, it may be better to explore trauma-based therapies in a professional setting. If, however, you have a sense that you know what your younger self needed not to close the construct, it may be helpful to jot it down in preparation for Technique 5.

One final note on the new frameworks. Given what we know about the plasticity of the neural system and that, when dysregulated, we can lay down new neural pathways, we may ask, Why shouldn't we rewrite history and lay down new pathways that tell us that nothing problematic ever happened to us? The first reason why this departure from reality is impossible is that neuronal pathways that were once activated may weaken in activation but can't be erased. There is no delete button for experience (other than severe brain damage). The second issue is psychological. Life is full of challenges, and we want our nervous system to be ready for them rather than pretend they don't exist. Even intrusive memories and continual "activations" by the unconscious mind are reminders that we have an old problem we haven't solved yet. Solving and processing it (backward) helps us meet daily life challenges in the present and the future with more resilience.

Designing the Relearning Experience

Now that we have found the significant events we want to work with and have explored new frameworks and experiences, we will try to design a technique that can reopen our closed constructs. Given you now know the necessary components for developmental relearning, each of you could potentially design a unique relearning experience that works best for you. However, if you would prefer a ready-made technique, we can combine beneficial aspects of different methods described by van der Kolk and offer a simple resource- and energy-efficient technique that leads to the reopening of our closed constructs.

Whereas we know that we could attempt to do the technique in our minds (imaginatively replaying events and applying new frameworks or experiences), in conversation with others (as in therapeutic situations or with supportive others), or even enacted nonverbally within a group therapy situation (as in Pesso-Boyden Psychomotor system), we will follow the example of psychologist James Pennebaker, whose "writing disclosure" intervention encouraged participants to go through this experience in writing. He asked people to write about their deepest thoughts and emotions regarding the most upsetting event in their lives for 15 minutes for 4 days. Studies show Pennebaker's intervention produced remarkable health, cognitive, and behavioral benefits.[23] Other than time and resource efficiency, externalizing language from the mind on paper (as in writing) allows an improved level of symbolic exploration and greater insight.[24] We only need one hour of time, privacy, and a pen and paper.

For what to write about, we will borrow insights from the Pesso-Boyden Psychomotor system, famous for its use of "structures," a form of group therapy in which the patients have physical "stand-ins" for those who were originally part of the significant event. For example, if Kai were to participate in one of these sessions, a therapeutic intervention would consist of a physical replaying of the scene, except that in addition to Kai's actual father, there would be another character who would "intervene" and provide Kai the support, protection, and affection he needed.[25] Whereas in the Pesso-Boyden system (which they aptly call "making new memories") everything is enacted physically, we will simulate the same experience in writing.

In addition to Pennebaker's and Pesso-Boyden's techniques, there are many more, as described by van der Kolk, that would be effective in completing the last exercise. You can choose from, or adapt, any of them in a way that works best for you.

In the next section, you can try a relearning technique that will blend the two strategies outlined in this chapter in the hope of distilling the experience necessary to update our closed constructs.

TECHNIQUE 5: RELEARNING

This is the final, and perhaps the most difficult, technique you will be asked to try. Remember that with self-guided techniques, you can continue or stop any time you want. Figure 6.1 and the following instructions will help guide you.

STEP 1: Find significant events you want to work with. *From the list of memories you have explored in Technique 4, choose the ones that* *are intrusive and emotionally charged. Place them in the first box of Figure 6.1.*

Example: Let's continue with the example from the last technique. Imagine we feel lonely and alienated, no matter how many people care for us. The memory that we were exploring in the example section of Technique 4 was coming home to an empty house and being there alone for a few hours. While exploring this memory, we realize it's also connected to the loss of our grandmother, who used to pick us up from school and stay with us until our parents would come back. We notice that this memory frequently pops up in our mind uninvited and that thinking about it makes us feel even more isolated and sad.

STEP 2: Find a new framework/experience. *Imagine your sibling, child, or a loved one was in the same situation; what would you tell them, or do, if you witnessed the situation? You can also imagine your adult self returning to your younger self and offering what you needed at the time not to overlearn. Jot down what you would tell your younger self in the second box of Figure 6.1. If you don't have a new framework for*

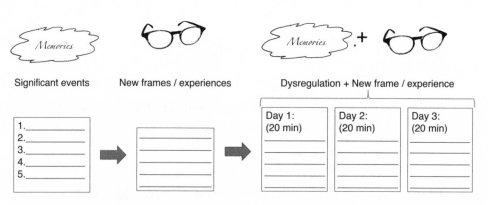

FIGURE 6.1 Technique 5: Relearning

understanding the situation, the significant event is too recent, or you don't feel safe, it may be best you skip this exercise.

Example: What would we have needed not to feel lonely and isolated in that situation? We would need an adult who would be present with us, who would tell us we are safe and protected, and who would help us understand that even if sometimes we are physically alone, we are still being loved and cared for by others. Another part of what we would have needed is someone to answer our questions about the loss of our grandmother. What happens to people when they die? If my parents die, would I be left all alone? We would have needed to know that death is a natural part of life, that we can still love people even when they are gone, and that if something happened to the parents, we'd still be safe and cared for.

STEP 3: Writing. *Go back to the situation you are working on and describe it in detail. You need to allow yourself to feel all the emotions you have had at the time of the event. (This activates the old, closed construct and provides necessary emotional dysregulation.) Once you finish describing it, you (your adult self) can walk onto the scene (with your younger self), intervene, and talk to the younger self and other "participants" of your significant event. You should try to ensure you don't "exit" the scene until your younger self feels safe, loved, supported, and protected. (This lays down new neural pathways, reopening the construct to new experience.)*

It's important to remember that this is an exercise in voluntary dysregulation, so that if at any point you feel too uncomfortable to proceed, you can just stop.

Finally, how would you know the exercise is working? On the third day, you may notice the emotional charge starting to dissipate as the construct is being updated. The memories of the event would then become descriptive, coherent, and "time-tagged"; that is, nonintrusive.

Example: The 20-minute writing exercise would look something like this: *"When I was 10, my grandmother died from a heart attack. Instead of her coming to pick me up from school, I'd go home alone. Once there, I'd lock all the doors and turn on the TV, but I still felt scared. I'd watch the clock, and if my parents were late from work, I thought something happened to them and that they were dead too. I'd feel so alone. If I could go back in time, I'd come into the living room, and just sit there with my little self; tell him that I'll be there with him, that he's protected and safe. I'd also tell him that although his parents are not there with him, they still love him and care for him. I'd also explain to him that sometimes people we love die, as Grandma did, but that's a natural part of life, and he can still love Grandma and feel her in his heart, even though she is gone. I'd give my little self a hug and tell him I love him and that he is safe."*

We'd continue writing in this way until the 20 minutes have passed. Then, the following two evenings, we'd repeat the exercise. We could start with the same words, or different ones—whatever comes to us in the moment.

STEP 4: Repeating the exercise with other significant events. *If you feel the exercise has worked for you, you can repeat it in turn with other significant events related either to the (a) same construct or (b) other constructs that are related to the want you are working on.*

Example: If the exercise was effective, we could repeat it on another related memory; for example, a memory of eating lunch alone at school while all the other kids were playing together. We'd then repeat steps 1–3 for as many memories as we listed in box 1 of Figure 6.1.

PART III

THE WHEEL
IN MOTION

CHAPTER SEVEN

CONCERTED ACTION

We grow and develop naturally, guided and pulled by our potential that manifests in our interests and things we love—whether ideas, skills, hobbies, careers, or people. This is why it's so painful when our development stalls or stops. When we work through each part of the Wheel of Self—motivation, behavior, emotions, mind, and the embodied past—it may seem fragmenting and difficult to understand how they all work together. Like a medical student who learns about all the body systems separately and then must step in front of a live patient, we now need to see what all our different parts of the self look like in motion.

PUTTING THE WHEEL INTO MOTION

Here in Figure 7.1 is our full set of tools that can help us move a stalled Wheel of Self.

We can enter the Wheel by experiencing issues with any part of the self. We may feel we can't reach our wants, no matter how hard we try, or that even when we achieve some important goals, we feel unfulfilled, not fully alive. We may be in burnout or exhausted from

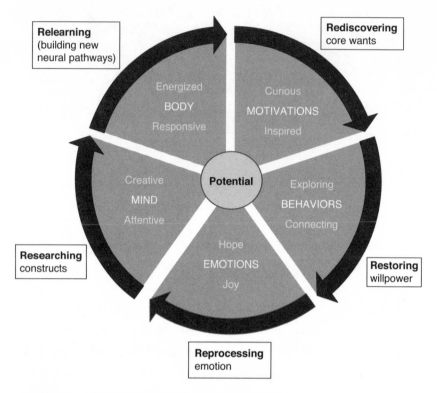

FIGURE 7.1   Tools for Working with the Wheel of Self

all the behavioral schedules we have built for ourselves that make our life into a sequence of tasks we feel good about only after we have completed them. We may struggle with difficult emotions that won't go away—recurrent shame, guilt, grief, resentment, or regret. We may be plagued with repetitive beliefs we know are detrimental to our lives, and yet can't help having them. And finally, we may be hurting from wounds inflicted a long time ago that we don't know what to do about. No matter what brings us to inner work, we can begin there.

Abhinav entered the Wheel in the Motivation section, not understanding why he kept trying and failing to achieve what should have been a simple want: working less. Kai felt exhausted by his diets and exercise regimes (behavior) and pursued by feelings of shame (emotion). Aisha was frustrated in her attempts to be assertive (behavior) and struggled with intrusive thoughts of not being good enough for a leadership position (mind). Emily experienced a lack of fulfillment and a feeling of not being fully alive (emotion). No matter where you enter the Wheel, you can explore it in a way that feels most natural to you. If you prefer more structure, you can follow this sequence of steps:

1. **Rediscovering our core wants: something about ourselves and not the world.** Aisha may have started wanting a promotion but understood she needed to work on valuing herself and feeling confident that she is good enough for what she wants to do. Kai began wanting his diet to "work" but realized that he needed to build a better relationship with his body first. Abhinav tried to work less and found he couldn't do it unless he found a way to build a loving relationship with his parents based on their present life rather than their past suffering. Emily didn't think she wanted anything (since she had reached all her goals) but realized she suppressed her core desire for creativity.

2. **Restoring willpower.** Without enough energy, we can't do the inner work. If we are exhausted, we will simply return to our old ways of doing things. Restoring willpower means discontinuing many of our energy-expensive behavioral "schedules," restoring ourselves better, reducing our distractors, and redirecting the willpower to work on inner change. While working on herself, Aisha stopped trying to implement the behavioral rules she forced on herself (such as speaking in each meeting at least three times or always leaving work last in the evening). Kai stopped his restrictive diets and gym schedules. Instead, they used their willpower to work around the Wheel of Self.

3. **Reprocessing emotion.** When we discontinue distractors and behavioral rules, we are bound to be faced with sticky emotions that have been overstaying their welcome and are signaling to us based on the old constructs. Only after Abhinav allowed himself to deeply experience his negative emotions did he realize he was plagued by feelings of guilt, which led him to insights about the true nature of his inability to work less. On the other hand, Kai had to learn that the continual feeling of shame he was experiencing was not just "who he is" but a result of his old constructs and early experiences, which could be changed.

4. **Researching cognitive constructs.** Once we know what negative emotions recur, we can find and explore old beliefs or closed constructs that continually activate the sticky emotions. Aisha's "I'm not good enough" and Emily's "I need to be financially secure to have the freedom to create" were constructs that closed under the stress of significant events. Being able to trace these constructs backward in history helped them prepare for the final technique.

5. **Relearning.** Here we find new frameworks and work on reopening and updating our old constructs with new experiences. This will recover and heal parts of the self that have long been left behind. Aisha, Emily, Kai, and Abhinav each had found a list of significant events that likely closed their constructs and worked through them with the relearning technique.

While this looks like a straightforward, linear sequence, sometimes we can go through different parts of a Wheel "in a flash"—that is, get an insight about an emotion, belief, or memory, without the laborious "working through." We are all experts on our own development; whatever sequence works best for us is the one to follow.

The test of how well our inner work "worked" is that we will feel fulfillment (motivation), restoration (behavior), temporary but not chronic negative emotions, realistic and updated constructs (mind), and normal memory storage of previously actively painful events (embodied past).

You may wonder why all techniques described in this book start with "re-": rediscovering, restoring, reprocessing, researching, and relearning. This is because the stalled parts of the self are locked in the past. Inner work is reworking the old problem so that the self can continue its development naturally.

Once the stalled Wheels of Self start moving, we may think we are finally done with our inner work. Yet, we will notice an interesting thing. We still want and strive, we still develop and grow, and we may still get stuck—on something else. Yet knowing how inner change works is less likely to leave us hopeless and resourceless. We can reapply the same techniques whenever our developmental momentum lags or stalls.

After Kai rebuilt a healthier relationship with his body, his relief from constant shame, disgust, and hopelessness resulted in him naturally caring for himself better. The relief and joy he felt were soon replaced by a new preoccupation. He realized that, though he was in his late twenties, he hadn't really dated much. He had always thought his weight was his barrier to dating, but now he realized he was missing the social skills necessary to build and maintain relationships. Even when he was around people who were attracted to him and he was attracted to, he felt awkward and anxious. Though this was upsetting to realize, Kai hadn't felt the hopelessness he was so used to feeling. Having once gone through the Wheel, he knew he could do it again if necessary.

Aisha left her organization within months of getting her Wheel of Self moving. Once she understood and felt her own value, and started trusting her intuition about her skills, the resentment at her bosses and colleagues was replaced by realistic anger at the injustice and prejudice she was experiencing. After a few conversations with her leaders that helped her understand they were not interested in changes she thought were necessary for her to stay, she found another, better, job in a competitor company. Once there, she realized she wanted to organize a mentorship group for women of color in her new organization, helping them navigate the inner and outer complexities they encounter in their professional life. Although it was scary to spearhead such an initiative, Aisha felt pulled by her mission and kept moving it forward, no matter how slow or difficult it seemed to her at the time.

Once Emily realized she didn't have to wait to explore her creativity, she started to paint again. To her distress, she found she didn't enjoy it as much as she did when she was younger. Instead, she started to explore other ways to engage her creativity. After some months of experimenting, Emily found out she loved writing fiction, romance novels in particular. In the beginning she felt so embarrassed that she kept it a secret even from her closest friends. Over time, though, with some more inner work on the closed construct of "My friends should admire me," she became more open about it. After a year she realized she liked writing enough to start cutting back on hours working at her company and giving more time to writing.

When Abhinav started working less, he thought all his other problems would resolve automatically. Though his relationship with his family improved noticeably, he realized that all the years he had been overworking had left his body in a rough shape. He used to fuel himself for long hours of work with unhealthy snacks, had irregular meals, and got very little sleep. With more time available, he thought it would be easy to improve his health. But he realized no matter how much time he had, his health wasn't improving. It turned out that Abhinav had learned to suppress signals of discomfort coming from his body since they were incompatible with the demands his job had on his time. He had ignored his body's messages for years, and even with much more time available, he didn't know how to stop ignoring them. Ironically, as a physiotherapist, he knew all he needed to do "in theory" that he wasn't doing in practice. He decided to focus on a new want: to reestablish a healthy connection to his body.

This is how most inner work ends: with wanting to fulfill another part of our potential and continuing to grow.

A LONG GAME

How do we keep growing given all the demands that are continually placed on us? While not easy, we can try to carve out space for self-development in our lives, and then use it wisely. Here are a few things you can do:

> **Find time.** Taking the time for inner work means we will have to be taking it from somewhere else. Most people have all crevices of their day filled with something they find either meaningful or necessary. Even when it's neither, it still seems difficult to give up. The suggestion here is to be aware of where we want to take time away from and do so with full consciousness of what we will lose and what we hope to gain.
>
> **Find space.** A little privacy—a closet, a laundry room, a corner in a coffee shop—will go a long way toward our self-development. Being around others, and even being reminded of them, while working on ourselves can pull us back into the roles and narratives we have been trying to maintain and away from the truthful vulnerability that is necessary to do the inner work.

Accept and then change. This is perhaps a paradoxical request—to accept ourselves as we are before we try to change. We may believe that the fastest and most energetic place from which to seek self-change is intense self-criticism or self-hatred. It turns out to be the opposite. Compassionate self-acceptance of our current state is the most elastic jumping board from which to leap toward self-development. We may ask, Why bother developing if we accept ourselves and are "fine"? Because we can accept our limitations today and want to develop beyond them tomorrow.

Don't get attached to your wounds. Many of us have found a way to live with our pains and fears, and even use them to motivate us to be accomplished and successful. As we work on healing, we may wonder whether, if we heal our wounds, there will be anything left to motivate us. If we feel our wounds made us successful, why let go of them? Because we can be motivated not just by fear but by exploration, curiosity, and interest. We will run fast both if we are running away from something dangerous and if we are running toward something we love. The only difference is that running *away* from something will take us to the first safe place, while running *toward* something will take us to our potential. We may let go of our wounds and still be proud of our scars while continuing to benefit from the resilience we built over the years.

Have patience. It's not easy to know ourselves, to understand all that's written between the covers of our book. Knowing the self can be more difficult than reading ancient texts written in some forgotten language. And unlike the books of old, we keep being written. Like learning a new language, it's work that benefits from patience.

While difficult to do, self-development is a long game. Whatever skills you learn once—how to find your core wants, restore yourself, process emotion, question your thoughts, or heal your wounds—you'll be able to practice and build on them as long as you breathe. True, self-development is tiring, is painful, requires courage, and is possibly the last thing you may want to do when feeling fragmented and pained. Yet it's also a way to fulfill your desires and get to feel the beauty of being whole. No one can do it for you. Only you can find an invisible thread of your potential that will keep pulling you forward. No matter how tired you may feel, it's still there, waiting for you.

I want to:
- Stop working compulsively and have time for relationships and health.
- Regain excitement about life.
- Make sure my parents are financially OK.
- I want to feel my life is mine to live, not always worried about everyone.

Distracting behaviors:
- Fantasize what I can get my parents with the money I make (better house, better car).
- Social media feeds.
- Check my bank accounts frequently.

Overdoing/forced behaviors:
- Work more when tired or stressed.
- Work nights.
- Work on a vacation.

I feel:
- Overwhelmed
- Anxious when not working
- Guilt
- Grief

My body memories:
- My Dad coming back from the night shift, overworked, his packed sandwich uneaten.
- When Dad injured his arm and couldn't work for two weeks, I heard my parents whispering about how much money there is left for food for the rest of the month.
- My parents getting me and my brother nice clothes and a backpack for school, although they never bought anything for themselves.

My thoughts:
- My parents worked hard all their lives for me and my brother, I'll never be able to repay their sacrifice.
- I should have helped them more when I was a kid.
- They sacrificed and overworked for me, it's my turn to sacrifice and overwork for them.
- I might as well work more, since at least that part of my life is going well.

Wheel of Self diagram with center labeled "Potential" surrounded by segments: MOTIVATION, BEHAVIOR, EMOTION, MIND, BODY.

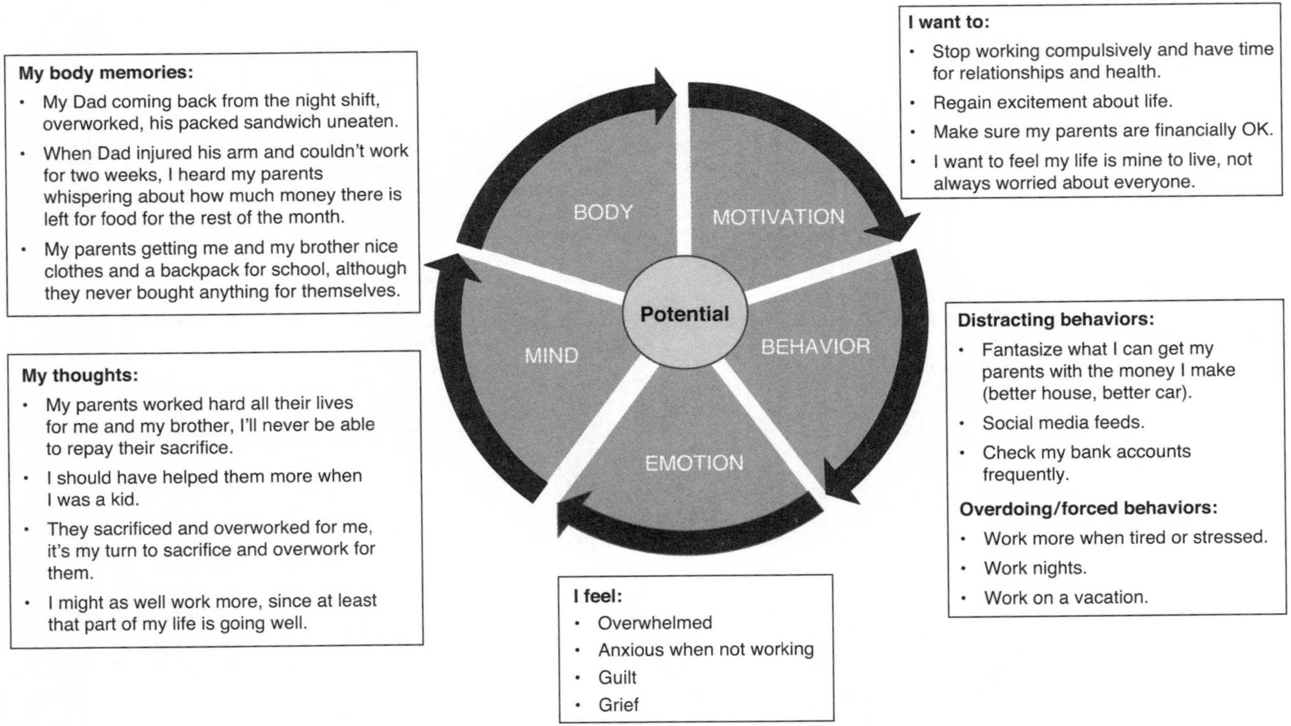

FIGURE A.1 Abhinav's Wheel of Self (Overworking)

I want:
- My body to be fit.
- My body to be healthy.
- My body to be lean.
- My body to be strong.

Distracting behaviors:
- Eat when stressed.
- Eat when already full.
- Eat when tired.
- Eat as a "reward" when I have to overwork.

Overdoing/forced behaviors:
- Yo-yo diets.
- Too strict exercise regimes.
- If I break the diet/routine even slightly, I abandon the diet/routine entirely.

I feel:
- Unattractive
- Disgusted
- Envious of fit others
- Hopeless
- Shame

My body memories:
- I ate sweets alone in front of the TV while waiting for my parents to return from work because I felt lonely and bored.
- Mother felt happiest cooking for me and the family and watching us eat.
- Mother fed me my favorite treats when I was upset.
- Father looked disgusted when he saw me change once.
- Father would wake me up at 6:00 a.m. to go exercise with him.
- Father took food off my plate during dinner.
- I was made fun of by classmates at school for being "chubby," all other kids laughing.
- At 10 YO, my cousin made fun of me because I ate two slices of cake at a birthday party.

My constructs:
- I am disgusting.
- I've always been bigger, and there's no point in trying to change it.
- If I don't eat everything my mother makes for me, she'll think I don't love her.
- I'm too busy to do something active every day.
- In old age, the body gets fat and saggy, there is nothing to be done about it.
- If I modify my cooking and eating habits, my social life will suffer.

Wheel diagram with center labeled "Potential" and segments: MOTIVATION, BEHAVIOR, EMOTION, MIND, BODY

FIGURE A.2 Kai's Wheel of Self (Poor Health and Fitness)

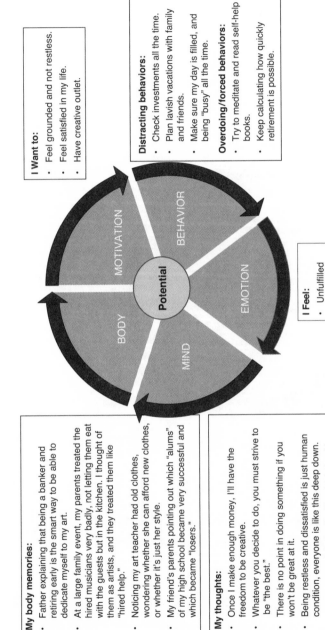

I Want to:
- Feel grounded and not restless.
- Feel satisfied in my life.
- Have creative outlet.

Distracting behaviors:
- Check investments all the time.
- Plan lavish vacations with family and friends.
- Make sure my day is filled, and being "busy" all the time.

Overdoing/forced behaviors:
- Try to meditate and read self-help books.
- Keep calculating how quickly retirement is possible.

I Feel:
- Unfulfilled
- Restless
- Frustrated
- Dissatisfied

My body memories:
- Father explaining that being a banker and retiring early is the smart way to be able to dedicate myself to my art.
- At a large family event, my parents treated the hired musicians very badly, not letting them eat with the guests but in the kitchen. I thought of them as artists, and they treated them like "hired help."
- Noticing my art teacher had old clothes, wondering whether she can afford new clothes, or whether it's just her style.
- My friend's parents pointing out which "alums" of my high school became very successful and which became "losers."

My thoughts:
- Once I make enough money, I'll have the freedom to be creative.
- Whatever you decide to do, you must strive to be "the best."
- There is no point in doing something if you won't be great at it.
- Being restless and dissatisfied is just human condition, everyone is like this deep down.
- I have a great job, family, friends, I should simply accept how I feel and be grateful for it.

FIGURE A.3 Emily's Wheel of Self (Unfulfilled Despite Success)

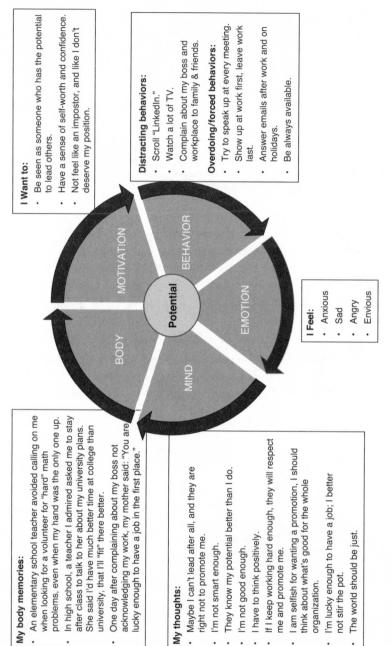

I Want to:
- Be seen as someone who has the potential to lead others.
- Have a sense of self-worth and confidence.
- Not feel like an impostor, and like I don't deserve my position.

Distracting behaviors:
- Scroll "LinkedIn."
- Watch a lot of TV.
- Complain about my boss and workplace to family & friends.

Overdoing/forced behaviors:
- Try to speak up at every meeting.
- Show up at work first, leave work last.
- Answer emails after work and on holidays.
- Be always available.

I Feel:
- Anxious
- Sad
- Angry
- Envious

My body memories:
- An elementary school teacher avoided calling on me when looking for a volunteer for "hard" math problems, even when my hand was the only one up.
- In high school, a teacher I admired asked me to stay after class to talk to her about my university plans. She said I'd have much better time at college than university, that I'll "fit" there better.
- One day after complaining about my boss not acknowledging my work, my mother said: "You are lucky enough to have a job in the first place."

My thoughts:
- Maybe I can't lead after all, and they are right not to promote me.
- I'm not smart enough.
- They know my potential better than I do.
- I'm not good enough.
- I have to think positively.
- If I keep working hard enough, they will respect me and promote me.
- I am selfish for wanting a promotion, I should think about what's good for the whole organization.
- I'm lucky enough to have a job; I better not stir the pot.
- The world should be just.

FIGURE A.4 Aisha's Wheel of Self (Unable to Advance Career)

NOTES

Introduction

1. Paul T. Costa Jr. and Robert R. McCrae, "Set like Plaster? Evidence for the Stability of Adult Personality," in *Can Personality Change?*, ed. Todd Heatherton and Joel Weinberger (Washington, DC: American Psychological Association, 1994), 21–40, https://doi.org/10.1037/10143-002.
2. Emma Goldberg, "The $2 Billion Question of Who You Are at Work," *New York Times*, March 5, 2023, https://www.nytimes.com/2023/03/05/business/remote-work-personality-tests.html.
3. Sanjay Srivastava et al., "Development of Personality in Early and Middle Adulthood: Set like Plaster or Persistent Change?," *Journal of Personality and Social Psychology* 84, no. 5 (2003): 1041–1053, https://doi.org/10.1037/0022-3514.84.5.1041.
4. Eberhard Fuchs and Gabriele Flügge, "Adult Neuroplasticity: More than 40 Years of Research," *Neural Plasticity* 2014 (2014): 541870, https://doi.org/10.1155/2014/541870.
5. Norman Doidge, *The Brain That Changes Itself: Stories of Personal Triumph from the Frontiers of Brain Science* (New York: Penguin Books, 2007).

Chapter One

1. Gabor Maté, *When the Body Says No: The Cost of Hidden Stress* (Toronto: Vintage Canada, 2003).
2. Bessel van der Kolk, *The Body Keeps the Score: Brain, Mind, and Body in the Healing of Trauma* (New York: Penguin Books, 2015).
3. William B. Swann Jr. and Stephen J. Read, "Self-Verification Processes: How We Sustain Our Self-Conceptions," *Journal of Experimental Social Psychology* 17, no. 4 (1981), 351–372, https://doi.org/10.1016/0022-1031(81)90043-3.

Chapter Two

1. David Schkade and Daniel Kahneman, "Does Living in California Make People Happy? A Focusing Illusion in Judgments of Life Satisfaction," *Psychological Science* 9, no. 5 (1998): 340–346, https://doi.org/10.1111/1467-9280.00066.
2. Philip Brickman, Dan Coates, and Ronnie Janoff-Bulman, "Lottery Winners and Accident Victims: Is Happiness Relative?," *Journal of Personality and Social Psychology* 36, no. 8 (1978): 917–927, https://psycnet.apa.org/doi/10.1037/0022-3514.36.8.917.
3. Silje Steinsbekk et al., "Emotional Feeding and Emotional Eating: Reciprocal Processes and the Influence of Negative Affectivity," *Child Development* 89, no. 4 (July/August 2017): 1234–1246, https://doi.org/10.1111/cdev.12756.
4. Geoff MacDonald and Mark R. Leary, "Why Does Social Exclusion Hurt? The Relationship between Social and Physical Pain," *Psychological Bulletin* 13, no. 2 (2005): 202–223, https://doi.org/10.1037/0033-2909.131.2.202.
5. Naomi I. Eisenberger, Matthew, D. Lieberman, and Kipling D. Williams, "Does Rejection Hurt? An fMRI Study of Social Exclusion," *Science* 302, no. 5643 (2003): 290–292, https://doi.org/10.1126/science.1089134.
6. C. Nathan DeWall, Geoff MacDonald, and Naomi I. Eisenberger, "Acetaminophen Reduces Social Pain: Behavioral and Neural Evidence," *Psychological Science* 21, no. 7 (2010): 931–937, https://doi.org/10.1177/0956797610374741.
7. Kyle G. Ratner, Amanda R. Kaczmarek, and Youngki Hong, "Can Over-the-Counter Pain Medications Influence Our Thoughts and Emotions?," *Policy Insights from the Behavioural and Brain Sciences* 5, no. 1 (2018): 82–89, https://doi.org/10.1177/2372732217748965.
8. Konrad Lorenz and Niko Tinbergen, "Taxis and Instinctive Action in Egg-Retrieving Behavior of the Greylag Goose," in *Instinctive Behavior: The Development of a Modern Concept,* ed. Claire H. Schiller (New York: University Press, 1957), 176–208.
9. Robert A. Emmons and Cheryl A. Crumpler, "Gratitude as a Human Strength: Appraising the Evidence," *Journal of Social and Clinical Psychology* 19, no. 1 (2000): 56–69, https://doi.org/10.1521/jscp.2000.19.1.56.
10. Charlotte van Oyen Witvliet et al., "Gratitude Predicts Hope and Happiness: A Two-Study Assessment of Traits and States," *The Journal of Positive Psychology* 14, no. 3 (2019): 271–282, https://doi.org/10.1080/17439760.2018.1424924.

Chapter Three

1. Raymond S. Nickerson, "How We Know—and Sometimes Misjudge—What Others Know: Imputing One's Own Knowledge to Others," *Psychological Bulletin* 125, no. 6 (1999): 737–759, https://psycnet.apa.org/doi/10.1037/0033-2909.125.6.737.
2. Bertram Gawronski, "Theory-Based Correction in Dispositional Inference: The Fundamental Attribution Error Is Dead, Long Live the Correspondence Bias," *European Review of Social Psychology* 15, no. 1 (2004): 183–217, https://doi.org/10.1080/10463280440000026.

3. Mark Muraven and Roy F. Baumeister, "Self-Regulation and Depletion of Limited Resources: Does Self-Control Resemble a Muscle?," *Psychological Bulletin* 126, no. 2 (2000): 247–259, https://psycnet.apa.org/doi/10.1037/0033-2909.126.2.247.

4. Roy Baumeister et al., "Ego Depletion: Is the Active Self a Limited Resource?," *Journal of Personality and Social Psychology* 74, no. 5 (1998): 1252–1265, https://doi.org/10.1037/0022-3514.74.5.1252.

5. Kathleen D. Vohs, Roy F. Baumeister, and Natalie J. Ciarocco, "Self-Regulation and Self-Presentation: Regulatory Resource Depletion Impairs Impression Management and Effortful Self-Presentation Depletes Regulatory Resources," *Journal of Personality and Social Psychology* 88, no. 4 (2005): 632–657, https://psycnet.apa.org/doi/10.1037/0022-3514.88.4.632.

6. Mark Muraven, Roy F. Baumeister, and Dianne M. Tice, "Longitudinal Improvement of Self-Regulation through Practice: Building Self-Control Strength through Repeated Exercise," *Journal of Social Psychology* 139, no. 4 (1999): 446–457, https://doi.org/10.1080/00224549909598404.

7. Jana Kühnel et al., "The Relevance of Sleep and Circadian Misalignment for Procrastination among Shift Workers," *Journal of Occupational and Organizational Psychology* 91, no. 1 (March 2018): 110–133, https://doi.org/10.1111/joop.12191.

8. Femke Beute and Yvonne A. W. de Kort, "Natural Resistance: Exposure to Nature and Self-Regulation, Mood, and Physiology after Ego-Depletion," *Journal of Environmental Psychology* 40 (December 2014): 167–178, https://doi.org/10.1016/j.jenvp.2014.06.004.

9. Dianne M. Tice et al., "Restoring the Self: Positive Affect Helps Improve Self-Regulation following Ego-Depletion," *Journal of Experimental Social Psychology* 43, no. 3 (May 2007): 379–384, https://doi.org/10.1016/j.jesp.2006.05.007.

10. Yi-Yuan Tang, Michael I. Posner, and Mary K. Rothbart, "Meditation Improves Self-Regulation over the Life Span," *Annals of the New York Academy of Sciences* 1307, no. 1 (2014): 104–111, https://doi.org/10.1111/nyas.12227.

11. Shaowei Xue, Yi-Yuan Tang, and Michael I. Posner, "Short-Term Meditation Increases Network Efficiency of the Anterior Cingulate Cortex," *NeuroReport* 22, no. 12 (August 2011): 570–574, https://doi.org/10.1097/WNR.0b013e328348c750.

12. Patrick M. Egan, Edward R. Hirt, and Samuel C. Karpen, "Taking a Fresh Perspective: Vicarious Restoration as a Means of Recovering Self-Control," *Journal of Experimental Social Psychology* 48, no. 2 (March 2012): 457–465, https://doi.org/10.1016/j.jesp.2011.10.019.

13. Veronika Job, Carol S. Dweck, and Gregory M. Walton, "Ego Depletion: Is It All in Your Head? Implicit Theories about Willpower Affect Self-Regulation," *Psychological Science* 21, no. 11 (November 2010): 1686–1693, https://doi.org/10.1177/0956797610384745.

14. Glen A. Nix et al., "Revitalization through Self-Regulation: The Effects of Autonomous and Controlled Motivation on Happiness and Vitality," *Journal of Experimental Social Psychology* 35 (May 1999): 266–284, https://doi.org/10.1006/jesp.1999.1382.

15. Edy Greenblatt, Michael Allan Kirk, and Erin V. Lehman, *Restore Yourself: The Antidote for Professional Exhaustion* (Los Angeles: Execu-Care Press, 2007).

16. "Career Burnout," The Centre for Addiction and Mental Health (CAMH), accessed April 18, 2023, https://www.camh.ca/en/camh-news-and-stories/career -burnout.

17. Yee Kong Chow et al., "Limbic Brain Structures and Burnout—A Systematic Review," *Advances in Medical Sciences* 63, no. 1 (March 2018): 192–198, https://doi .org/10.1016/j.advms.2017.11.004.

18. Gabor Maté, *When the Body Says No: The Cost of Hidden Stress* (Toronto: Vintage Canada, 2004).

19. Sheina Orbell and Bas Verplanken, "The Automatic Component of Habit in Health Behavior: Habit as Cue-Contingent Automaticity," *Health Psychology* 29, no. 4 (2010): 374–383, https://psycnet.apa.org/doi/10.1037/a0019596.

20. Ellen J. Langer and Mihnea C. Moldoveanu, "The Construct of Mindfulness," *Journal of Social Issues* 56, no. 1 (Spring 2000): 1–9, https://doi.org/10.1111/0022 -4537.00148.

21. Ellen J. Langer, *Counterclockwise: Mindful Health and the Power of Possibility* (New York: Ballantine Books, 2009).

22. Ellen J. Langer, "Matters of Mind: Mindfulness/Mindlessness in Perspective," *Consciousness and Cognition* 1, no. 3 (September 1992): 289–305, https://doi.org /10.1016/1053-8100(92)90066-J.

23. Alia Crum and Christopher Lyddy, "De-stressing Stress: The Power of Mindsets and the Art of Stressing Mindfully," in *The Wiley Blackwell Handbook of Mindfulness,* ed. Amanda Ie, Christelle T. Ngnoumen, and Ellen J. Langer (Hoboken, NJ: Wiley-Blackwell, 2014).

24. Ellen J. Langer et al., "Two New Applications of Mindlessness Theory: Alcoholism and Aging," *Journal of Aging Studies* 2, no. 3 (Autumn 1988): 289–299, https://doi.org/10.1016/0890-4065(88)90008-4.

25. Charles N. Alexander et al., "Transcendental Meditation, Mindfulness, and Longevity: An Experimental Study with the Elderly," *Journal of Personality and Social Psychology* 57, no. 6 (1989): 950–964, https://doi.org/10.1037/0022-3514.57 .6.950.

26. Francesco Pagnini et al., "Mindfulness, Physical Impairment and Psychological Well-Being in People with Amyotrophic Lateral Sclerosis," *Psychology & Health* 30, no. 5 (October 2014): 503–517, https://doi.org/10.1080/08870446.2014 .982652.

Chapter Four

1. Nico H. Frijda, *The Laws of Emotion* (Mahwah, NJ: Erlbaum, 2007).

2. Nathan J. Emery et al., "The Effects of Bilateral Lesions of the Amygdala on Dyadic Social Interactions in Rhesus Monkeys (Macaca Mulatta)," *Behavioral Neuroscience* 115, no. 3 (2001): 515–544, https://psycnet.apa.org/doi/10.1037/0735 -7044.115.3.515.

3. Rupa Gupta et al., "The Amygdala and Decision-Making," *Neuropsychologia* 49, no. 4 (March 2011): 760–766, https://doi.org/10.1016/j.neuropsychologia.2010 .09.029.

4. Keith Oatley and Philip N. Johnson-Laird, "Towards a Cognitive Theory of Emotions," *Cognition and Emotion* 1, no. 1 (1987): 29–50, https://doi.org/10.1080/02699938708408362.

5. Amy F. T. Arnsten et al., "The Effects of Stress Exposure on Prefrontal Cortex: Translating Basic Research into Successful Treatments for Post-Traumatic Stress Disorder," *Neurobiology of Stress* 1 (January 2015): 89–99, https://doi.org/10.1016/j.ynstr.2014.10.002.

6. Brad J. Bushman, "Does Venting Anger Feed or Extinguish the Flame? Catharsis, Rumination, Distraction, Anger, and Aggressive Responding," *Personality and Social Psychology Bulletin* 28, no. 6 (June 2002): 724–731, https://doi.org/10.1177/0146167202289002.

Chapter Five

1. Nelson Cowan, "George Miller's Magical Number of Immediate Memory in Retrospect: Observations on the Faltering Progression of Science," *Psychological Review* 122, no. 3 (2015): 536–541, https://psycnet.apa.org/doi/10.1037/a0039035.

2. Fernand Gobet and Herbert A. Simon, "Expert Chess Memory: Revisiting the Chunking Hypothesis," *Memory* 6, no. 3 (1998): 225–255, https://doi.org/10.1080/741942359.

3. Hans Gelter, "Why is reflective thinking uncommon?," *Reflective Practice* 4, no. 3, (2003): 337–344, https://doi.org/10.1080/1462394032000112237.

4. Gelter, "Why is reflective thinking uncommon," 341.

5. Peter M. Gollwitzer and John A. Bargh, "Automaticity in Goal Pursuits" in *Handbook of Competence and Motivation*, ed. Andrew J. Elliot, (New York: Guilford Press, 2005): 624–646.

6. Deirdre Barrett, "Dreams and Creative Problem-Solving," *Annals of the New York Academy of Sciences* 1406, no. 1 (October 2017): 64–67, https://doi.org/10.1111/nyas.13412.

7. Ellen J. Langer, *Mindfulness* (Boston: Addison Wesley, 1989).

8. Daniel T. Gilbert, Douglas S. Krull, and Patrick S. Malone, "Unbelieving the Unbelievable: Some Problems in the Rejection of False Information," *Journal of Personality and Social Psychology* 59, no. 4, (1990): 601–613, https://psycnet.apa.org/doi/10.1037/0022-3514.59.4.601.

9. Ap Dijksterhuis et al., "On Making the Right Choice: The Deliberation-without-Attention Effect," *Science* 311, no. 5763 (2006): 1005–1007, https://doi.org/10.1126/science.1121629.

10. Daniel Kahneman, *Thinking, Fast and Slow* (New York: Farrar, Straus and Giroux, 2011).

11. Nicolas Porot and Eric Mandelbaum, "The Science of Belief: A Progress Report," *Wiley Interdisciplinary Reviews: Cognitive Science* 12, no. 2 (March/April 2021): 1539, https://doi.org/10.1002/wcs.1539.

12. Timothy C. Brock and Joe L. Balloun, "Behavioral Receptivity to Dissonant Information," *Journal of Personality and Social Psychology* 6, no. 4 (1967): 413–428, https://psycnet.apa.org/doi/10.1037/h0021225.

Chapter Six

1. John Bowlby, *A Secure Base* (London: Routledge, 2005), https://doi.org/10.4324
/9780203440841.
2. Basira Salehi, M. Isabel Cordero, and Carmen Sandi, "Learning Under Stress:
The Inverted-U-Shape Function Revisited," *Learning and Memory* 17, (2010):
522–530, http://www.learnmem.org/cgi/doi/10.1101/lm.1914110.
3. James McGaugh and Benno Roozendaal, "Role of Adrenal Stress Hormones in
Forming Lasting Memories in the Brain," *Current Opinion in Neurobiology* 12,
no. 2 (April 2002): 205–210, https://doi.org/10.1016/S0959-4388(02)00306-9.
4. Benno Roozendaal, Bruce S. McEwen, and Sumantra Chattarji, "Stress, Memory, and the Amygdala," *Nature Reviews Neuroscience* 10 (May 2009): 423–433,
https://doi.org/10.1038/nrn2651.
5. David Finkelhor, "Trends in Adverse Childhood Experiences (ACEs) in the
United States," *Child Abuse & Neglect* 108 (October 2020): 104641, https://doi
.org/10.1016/j.chiabu.2020.104641.
6. George W. Brown and Tirril Harris, *Social Origins of Depression: A Study of Psy-
chiatric Disorder in Women* (London: Tavistock, 1978).
7. George A. Bonanno, "Loss, Trauma, and Human Resilience: Have We Underes-
timated the Human Capacity to Thrive after Extremely Aversive Events?," *American Psychologist* 59, no. 1 (2004): 20–28, https://doi.org/10.1037/0003-066X.59
.1.20.
8. Richard G. Tedeschi and Lawrence G. Calhoun, "Posttraumatic Growth: Con-
ceptual Foundations and Empirical Evidence," *Psychological Inquiry* 15, no. 1
(2004): 1–18, https://doi.org/10.1207/s15327965pli1501_01.
9. Per Bak and Kan Chen, "Self-Organized Criticality," *Scientific American* 264,
no. 1 (January 1991): 46–53, http://www.jstor.org/stable/24936753.
10. Katie Witkiewitz and G. Alan Marlatt, "Modeling the Complexity of Post-
Treatment Drinking: It's a Rocky Road to Relapse," *Clinical Psychology Review*
27, no. 6 (July 2007): 724–738, https://doi.org/10.1016/j.cpr.2007.01.002.
11. Adele M. Hayes et al., "Change is Not Always Linear: The Study of Nonlinear
and Discontinuous Patterns of Change in Psychotherapy," *Clinical Psychology Review* 27, no. 6 (July 2007): 715–723, https://doi.org/10.1016/j.cpr.2007.01.008.
12. R. R. Vallacher, S. J. Read, and A. Nowak, "The Dynamical Perspective in Personality and Social Psychology," *Personality and Social Psychology Review* 6 (2002):
264–273, https://doi.org/10.1207/S15327957PSPR0604_01.
13. Jennifer L. Pals and Dan P. McAdams, "The Transformed Self: A Narrative Understanding of Posttraumatic Growth," *Psychological Inquiry* 15, no. 1 (2004):
65–69, https://www.jstor.org/stable/20447204.
14. Arnold van Gennep, *The Rites of Passage* (Chicago: The University of Chicago
Press, 2019).
15. Robert Jay Lifton, *Thought Reform and the Psychology of Totalism: A Study of
"Brainwashing" in China* (Chapel Hill, NC: University of North Carolina Press,
1989).

16. Aldo Cimino, "The Evolution of Hazing: Motivational Mechanisms and the Abuse of Newcomers," *Journal of Cognition and Culture* 11, no. 3–4 (2011): 241–267, https://doi.org/10.1163/156853711X591242.

17. Bessel A. van der Kolk, *The Body Keeps the Score: Brain, Mind, and Body in the Healing of Trauma* (New York: Viking Penguin, 2014).

18. James W. Pennebaker and John F. Evans, *Expressive Writing: Words That Heal* (Bedford, IN: Idyll Arbor Inc, 2014).

19. van der Kolk, *The Body Keeps the Score*, 241–308.

20. Daniel L. Schacter, "The Seven Sins of Memory: Insights from Psychology and Cognitive Neuroscience," *American Psychologist* 54, no. 3 (1999): 182–203, https://psycnet.apa.org/doi/10.1037/0003-066X.54.3.182.

21. Bessel A. van der Kolk and Rita Fisler, "Dissociation and the Fragmentary Nature of Traumatic Memories: Overview and Exploratory Study," *Journal of Traumatic Stress* 8, no. 4 (October 1995): 505–525, https://doi.org/10.1007/BF02102887.

22. Julie Krans et al., "Intrusive Trauma Memory: A Review and Functional Analysis," *Applied Cognitive Psychology* 23, no. 8 (November 2009): 1076–1088, https://doi.org/10.1002/acp.1611.

23. Pennebaker and Evans, *Expressive Writing*.

24. Keith Oatley and Maja Djikic, "Writing as Thinking," *Review of General Psychology* 12, no. 1 (2008): 9–27, https://doi.org/10.1037/1089-2680.12.1.9.

25. van der Kolk, *The Body Keeps the Score*.

ACKNOWLEDGMENTS

An idea doesn't arise in a vacuum—it originates from ideas that came before. I'd like to start, then, by thanking those whose minds helped shape mine. Without their ideas, friendship, and mentorship, I couldn't have envisioned what became this book. I feel deepest gratitude to Keith Oatley, who listened to every idea, read every draft, coaxed, supported, and helped in all the ways a novice writer needs to bring a book into the world. Mihnea C. Moldoveanu brought me from the world of academic abstractions into the real world, to Rotman School of Management, and envisioned and built a unique space (The Self-Development Laboratory) where we help real people make meaningful changes in their lives. Ellen J. Langer inspired me (as she does countless others) with her brilliance and generosity. Finally, J. B. Peterson's patience in supervising my PhD (whose topic varied wildly from one year to the next) helped me find what interested me the most—how adults grow.

To my students, thank you for asking for this book. You are the reason I wrote it, and your questions sharpened my thinking. Whenever I was in doubt, I'd ask myself, What would they find most useful? and the answer would keep me writing.

I'm grateful to my agent Linda Konner, editors Sarah Modlin and Neal Maillet, and the wonderful team at Berrett-Koehler Publishers (whose author-centric approach to publishing exceeded my wildest expectations). Thank you for taking a chance on me and the book.

I am blessed with a network of supporters—including friends, family, and loved ones—all those who read snippets large and small, opined about ideas, phrases, and titles, and had to listen to me go on and on about the book for the last seven years. Thank you.

INDEX

ABOUT THE AUTHOR

Photo by Caroline Lessa

Maja Djikic, PhD, is an associate professor of organizational behavior and human resource management, the director of The Self-Development Laboratory, and the academic director of the Rotman Executive Coaching Certificate program at the Rotman School of Management, University of Toronto. She is a teaching fellow at The Institute for Gender and the Economy. As a psychologist specializing in the field of personality development, Dr. Djikic examines the processes and methods of developing a balanced and flexible self. She has published more than 35 scientific articles and book chapters on personality development, and her research has been featured in over 50 media outlets (including the *New York Times*, *Salon*, *Slate*, and *Scientific American Mind*) in 15 countries. In addition to teaching MBA students at Rotman, she teaches leaders in the Executive MBA program and custom executive programs. Her government and corporate clients have included Health Ontario, United Health Network, McKinsey & Co., Deloitte, Eli Lilly, CSL Behring, Sun Life Financial, Royal Bank of Canada, TD Bank, Aird & Berlis LLP, Hyundai Canada, Microsoft, Alcon, Right to Play, Open Text, Reach Out Centre for Kids, Loblaws Inc., and Capital One.

Dear reader,

Thank you for picking up this book and welcome to the worldwide BK community! You're joining a special group of people who have come together to create positive change in their lives, organizations, and communities.

What's BK all about?

Our mission is to connect people and ideas to create a world that works for all.

Why? Our communities, organizations, and lives get bogged down by old paradigms of self-interest, exclusion, hierarchy, and privilege. But we believe that can change. That's why we seek the leading experts on these challenges—and share their actionable ideas with you.

A welcome gift

To help you get started, we'd like to offer you a **free copy** of one of our bestselling ebooks:

www.bkconnection.com/welcome

When you claim your **free ebook**, you'll also be subscribed to our blog.

Our freshest insights

Access the best new tools and ideas for leaders at all levels on our blog at ideas.bkconnection.com.

Sincerely,

Your friends at Berrett-Koehler

Certified

Corporation